# FAMOUS RAPES

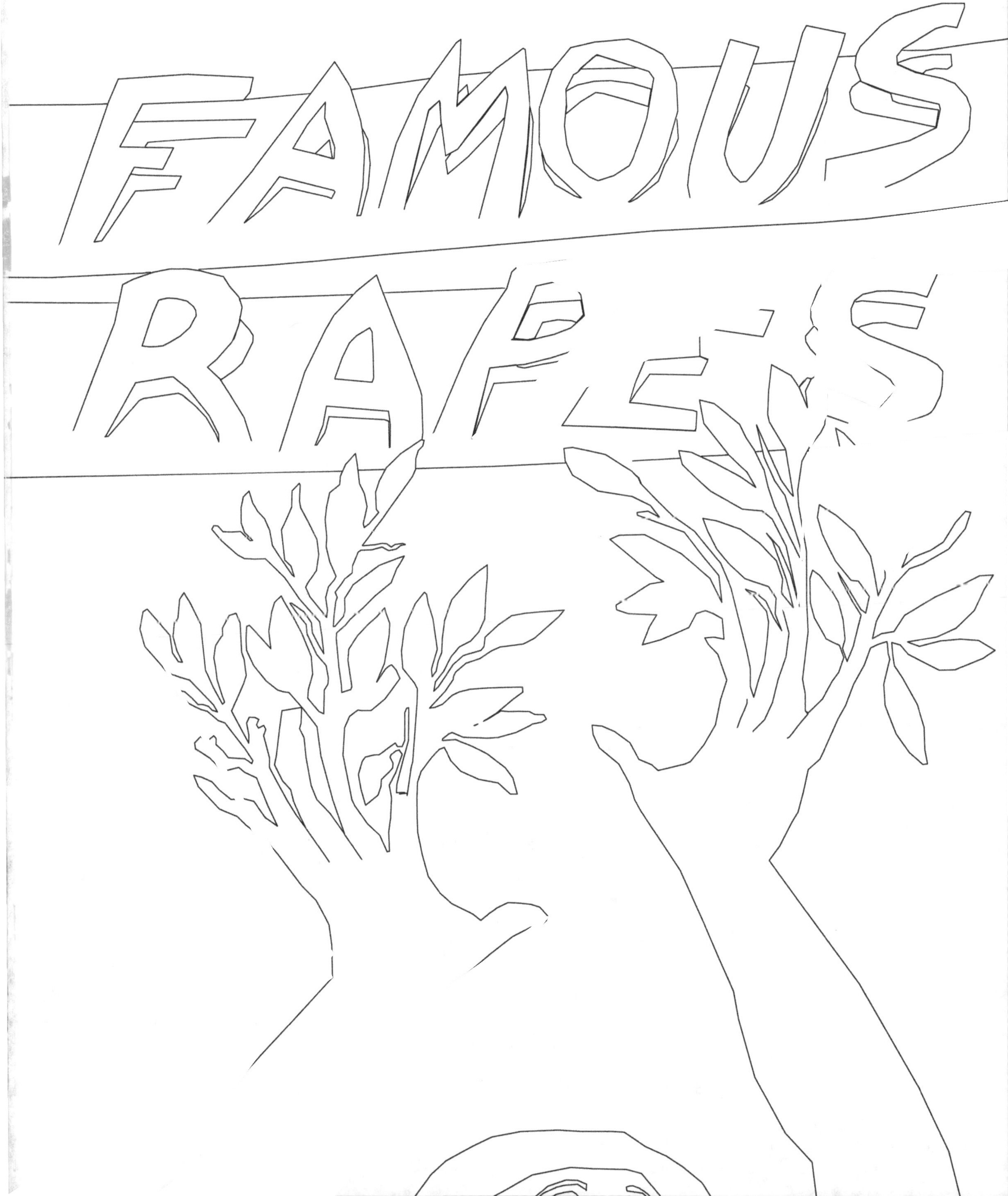

Famous Rapes: The Coloring Book

Author: Andrea Baker
Copyright by Andrea Baker, 2018 - All Rights Reserved.

All rights reserved, including the right to reproduce this book in whole or in part.
For information, contact Water Street Press at www.waterstreetpressbooks.com.

This is a Water Street Press edition, 2018 Designer Credits

Cover Art by Sally Eckhoff

Author Photo by Dietmar Busse

Interior Design by Thomson-Shore, Inc.

Library of Congress Cataloging-in-Publication Data is available.

ISBN: 978-1-62134-224-3

Author's Note:
# AN INVITATION TO HOPE

The Western world is currently at work addressing and reconciling with sexually predatory behaviors. Those behaviors are a manifestation of the trace of history that is still at work in society today. Historically, if the vulnerable could be of utility to those who held power, they were considered fair game. That utility took the shape of pyramids built by slaves, the shape of imperialism, and the shape of sexual assault.

I like breaking things down to shapes. Once upon a time, I was searching for the shapes that represented my own experiences. I was interested in shapes for grief, for abuse, and for resilience and hope. I have a background in art history, so when I began to think about the shapes for assault, Old Master paintings came to mind—and they explained a lot.

I saw that behaviors that are condemned now were celebrated then. The story of the founding of Rome is that the men had no women of their own, so they captured some women from the neighboring tribe. This bride-capture event, The Rape of the Sabine Women, was celebrated as a passionate rapture by the painters of the Renaissance. The same painters also gravitated to the shape of Lucretia. She committed suicide after a sexual assault. In the paintings, her suicide is honorable—the right thing to do.

There are setbacks along the way, but history, in sum, is a story of progress. Attitudes have shifted away from allowing unchecked power to the few; laws have been re-written to protect women, people of color, disabled people, and the earth itself. The intrinsic value of women's autonomy and agency is thought of today in a way that would seem absurd to even recent generations. Still, the trace of our long history lives in abusive behaviors and in our most private shame. Our survivors still cope with the same self-blame that Lucretia acted out.

My interest is in the shape of history unfurling. What I want to examine is how our human past informs our presumptions, which manifest both as abusive behaviors, and as the widespread ignoring of abusive behaviors. It soothes me to understand how we got to a world where the media buzzes with allegations of sexual assault. Behaviors that were overtly, then covertly, allowed are less and less OK.

Understanding the course of history allows us to move past our residual tolerance for violence, and past shame and despair. We all participate in the progress of history by addressing its shapes, giving them different colors, and inviting new possibilities. Famous Rapes—and Famous Rapes: The Coloring Book—is an invitation to hope.

Andrea Baker
November 2017

# TEST YOUR COLORS
# ON THESE IMAGES OF HOPE.

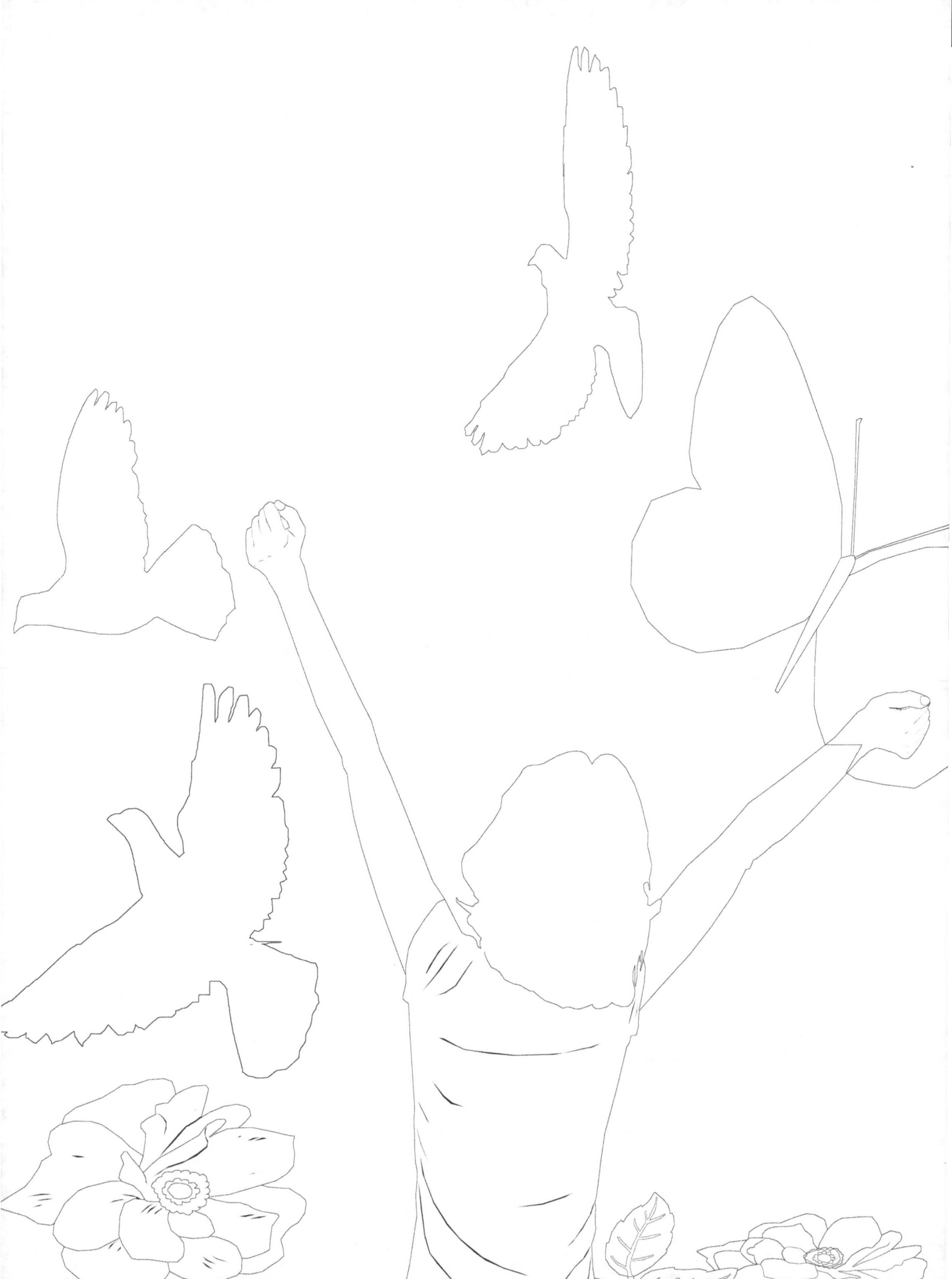

# ONCE UPON A TIME....

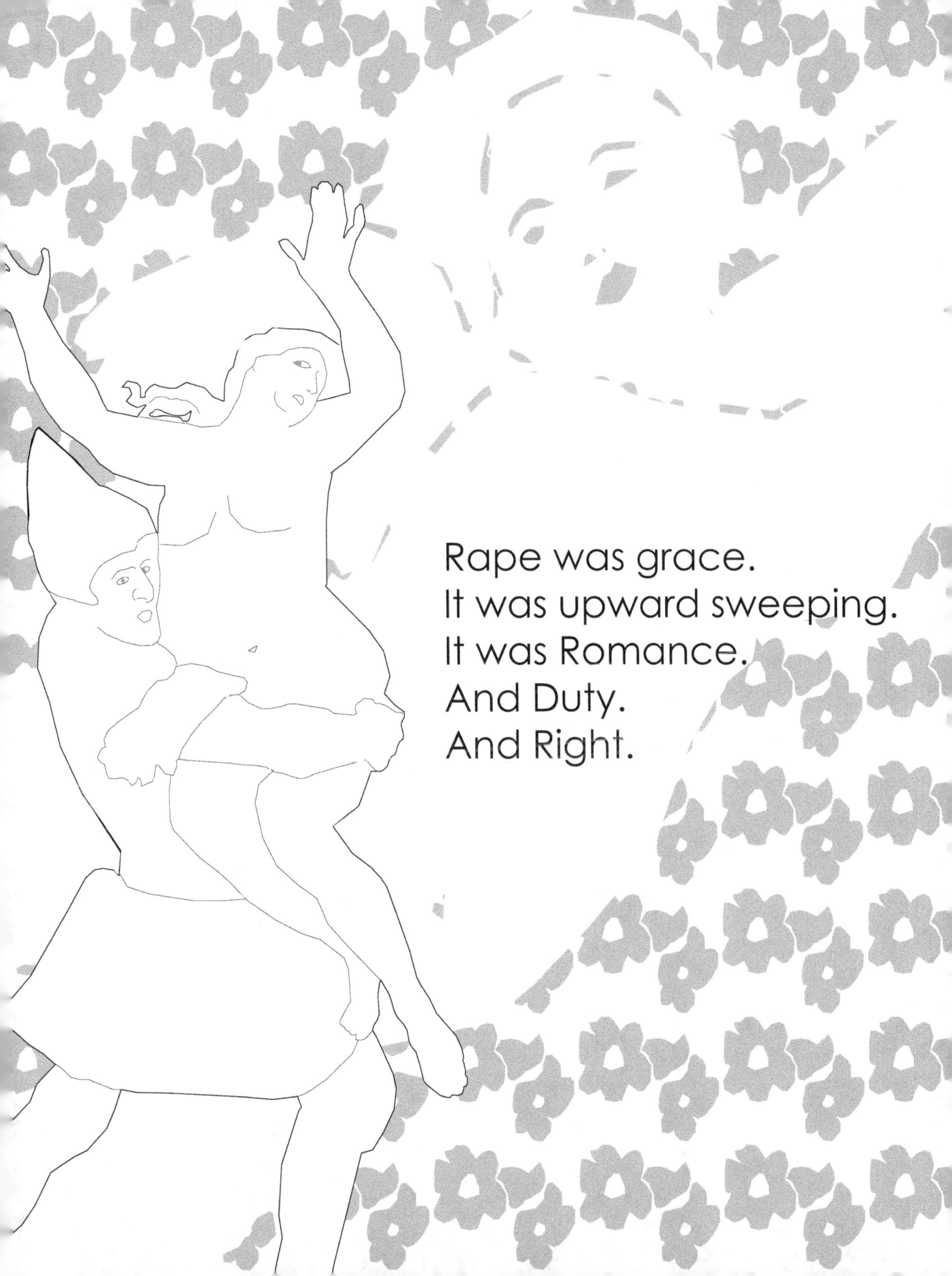

Rape was grace.
It was upward sweeping.
It was Romance.
And Duty.
And Right.

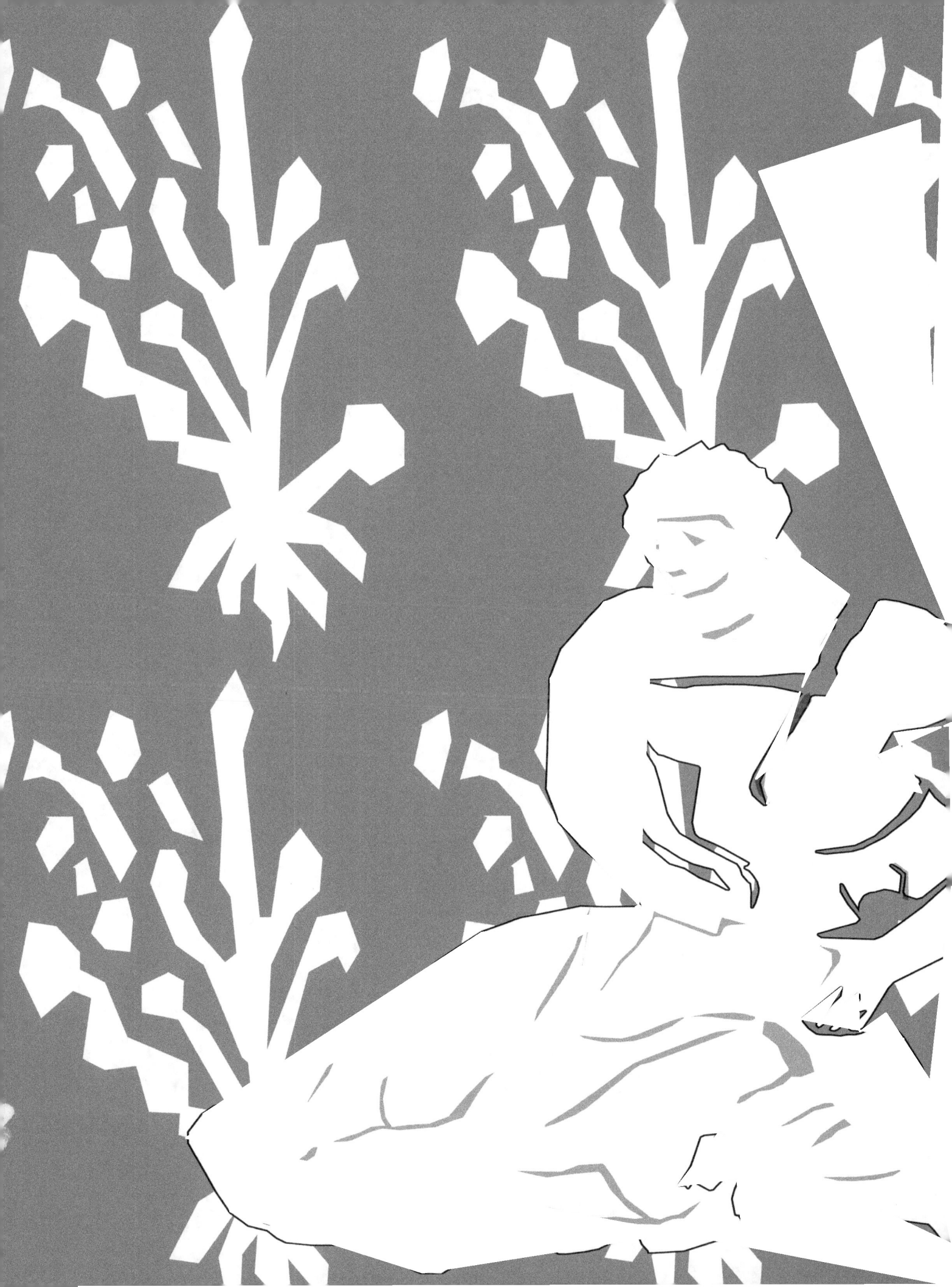

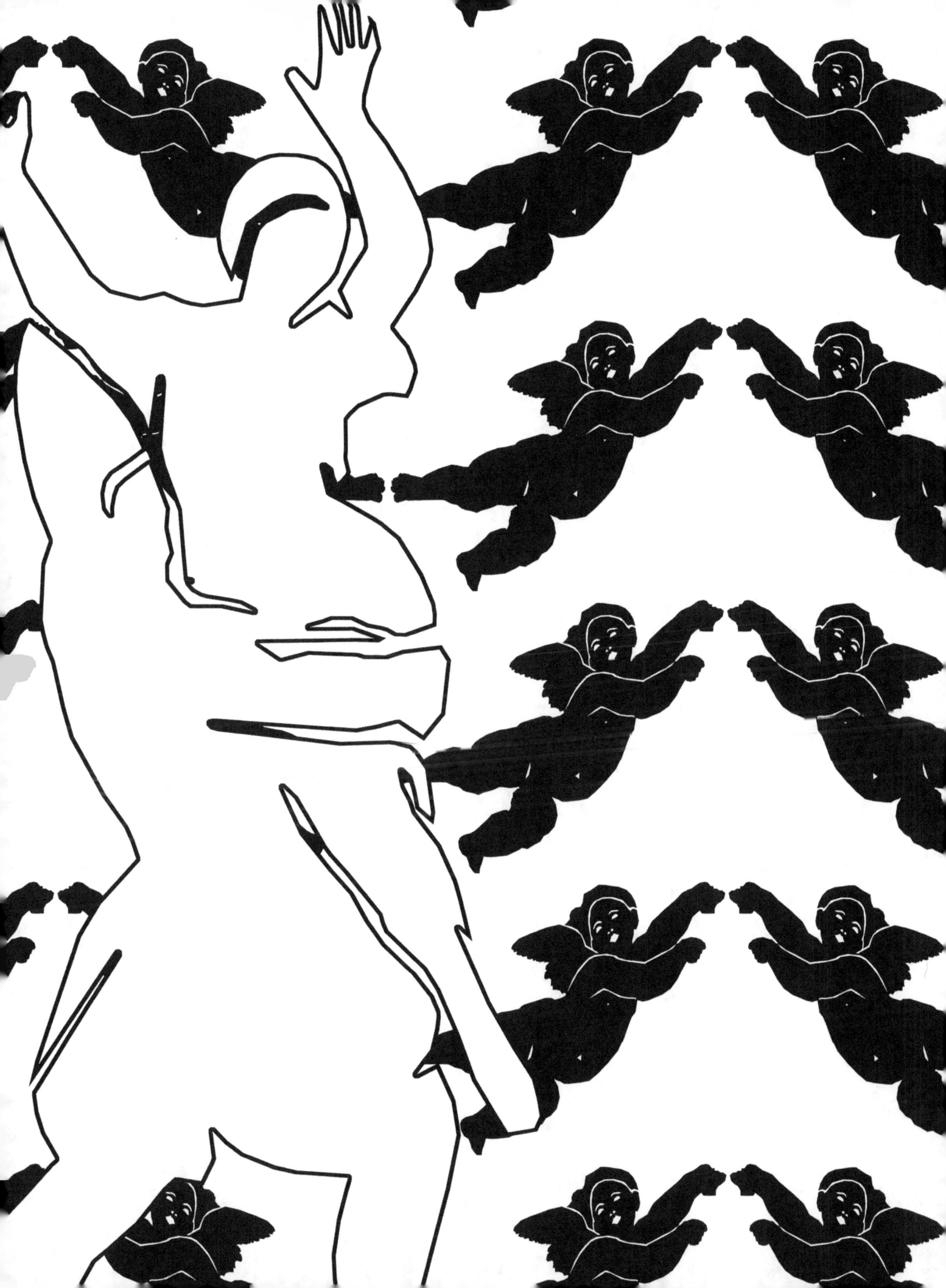

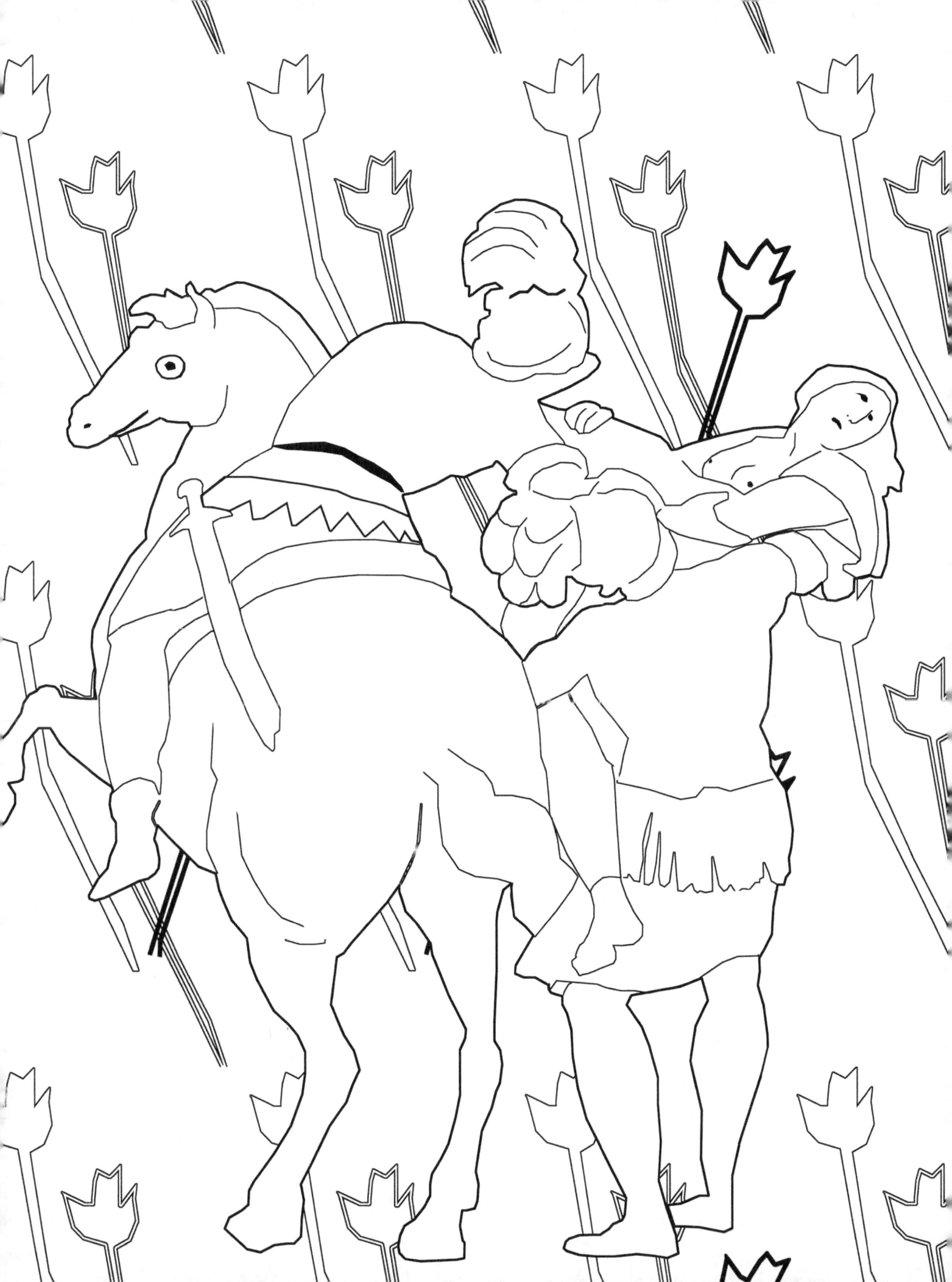

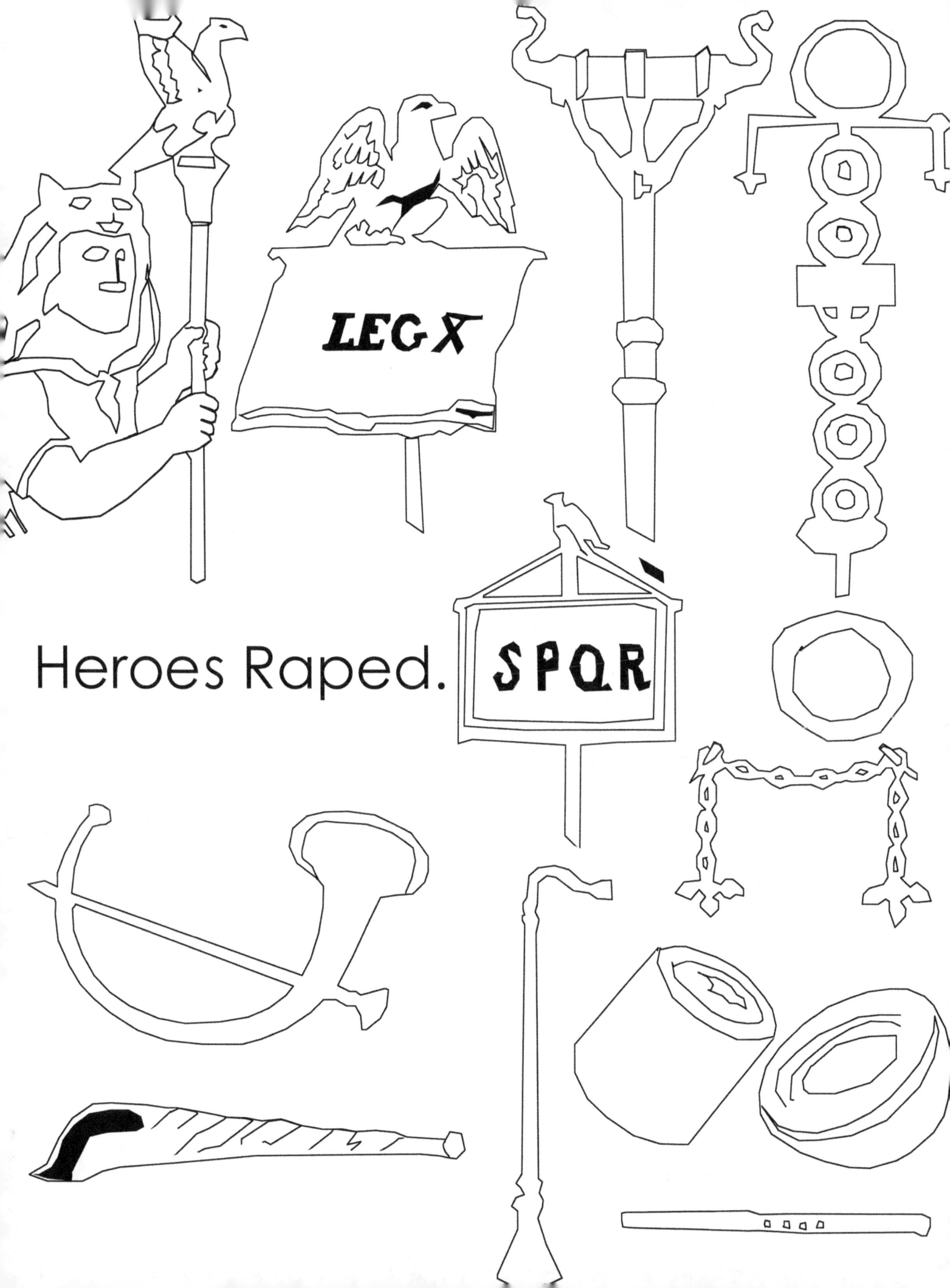

Heroes Raped.

LEG X

SPQR

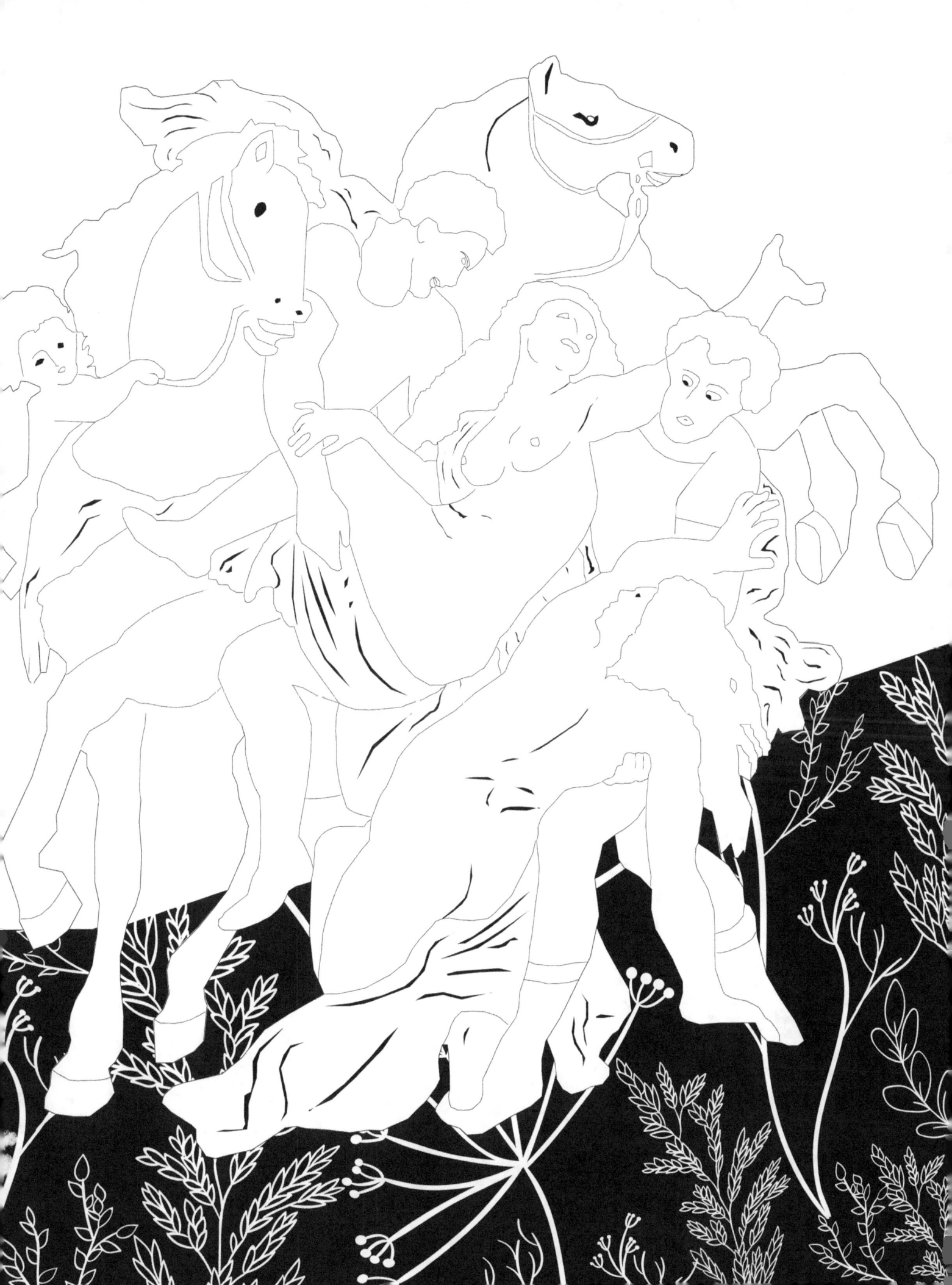

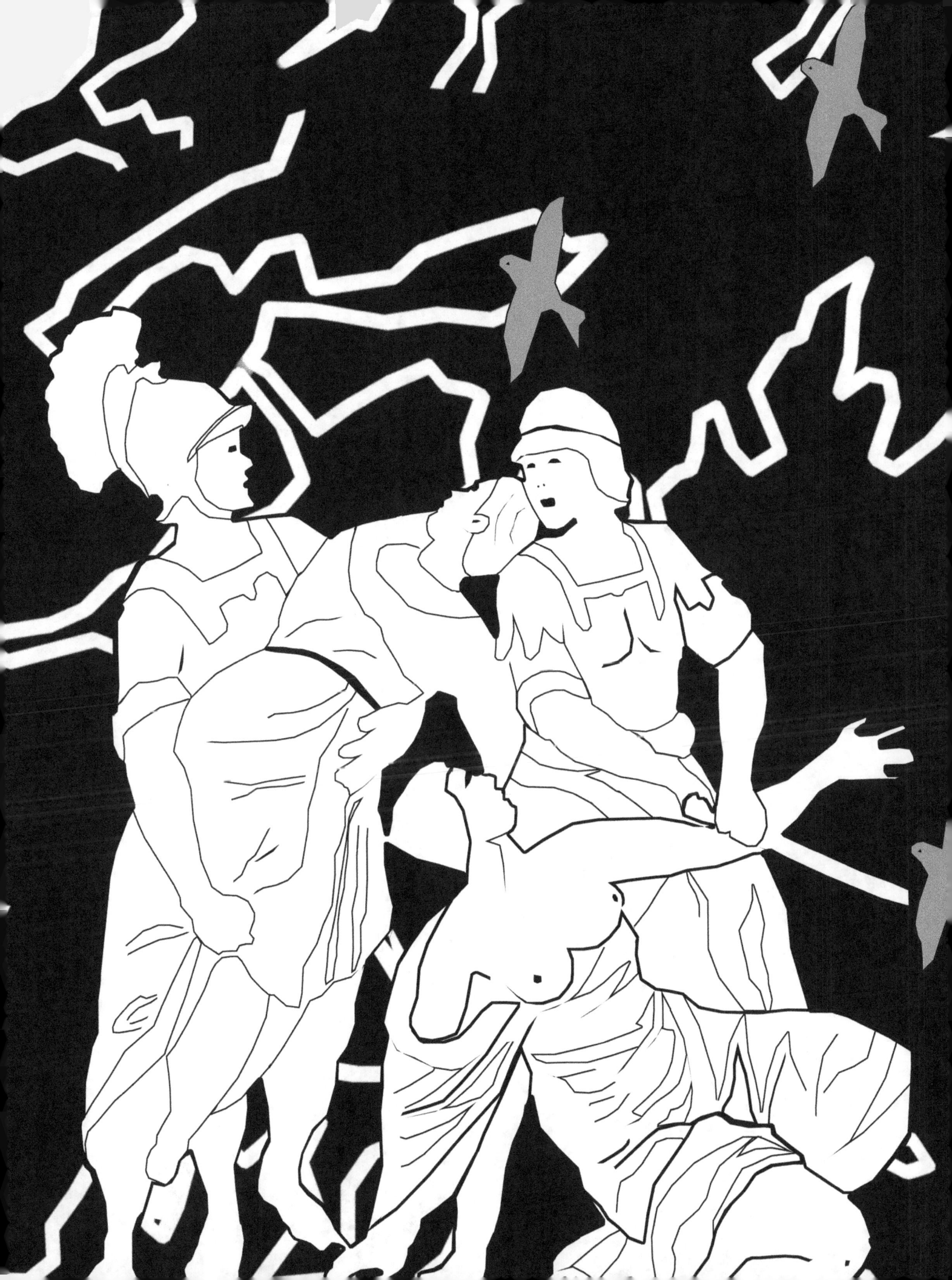

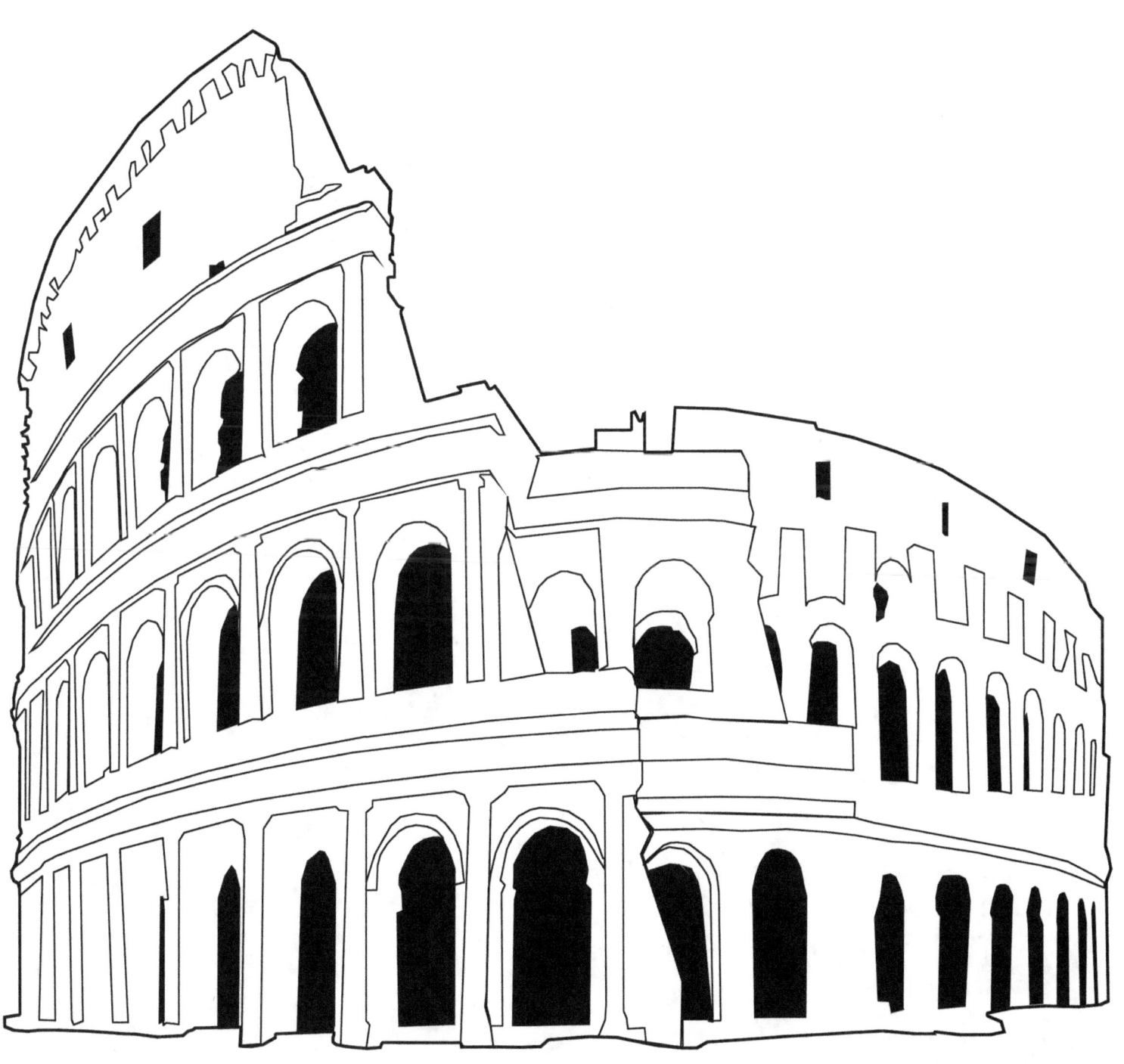

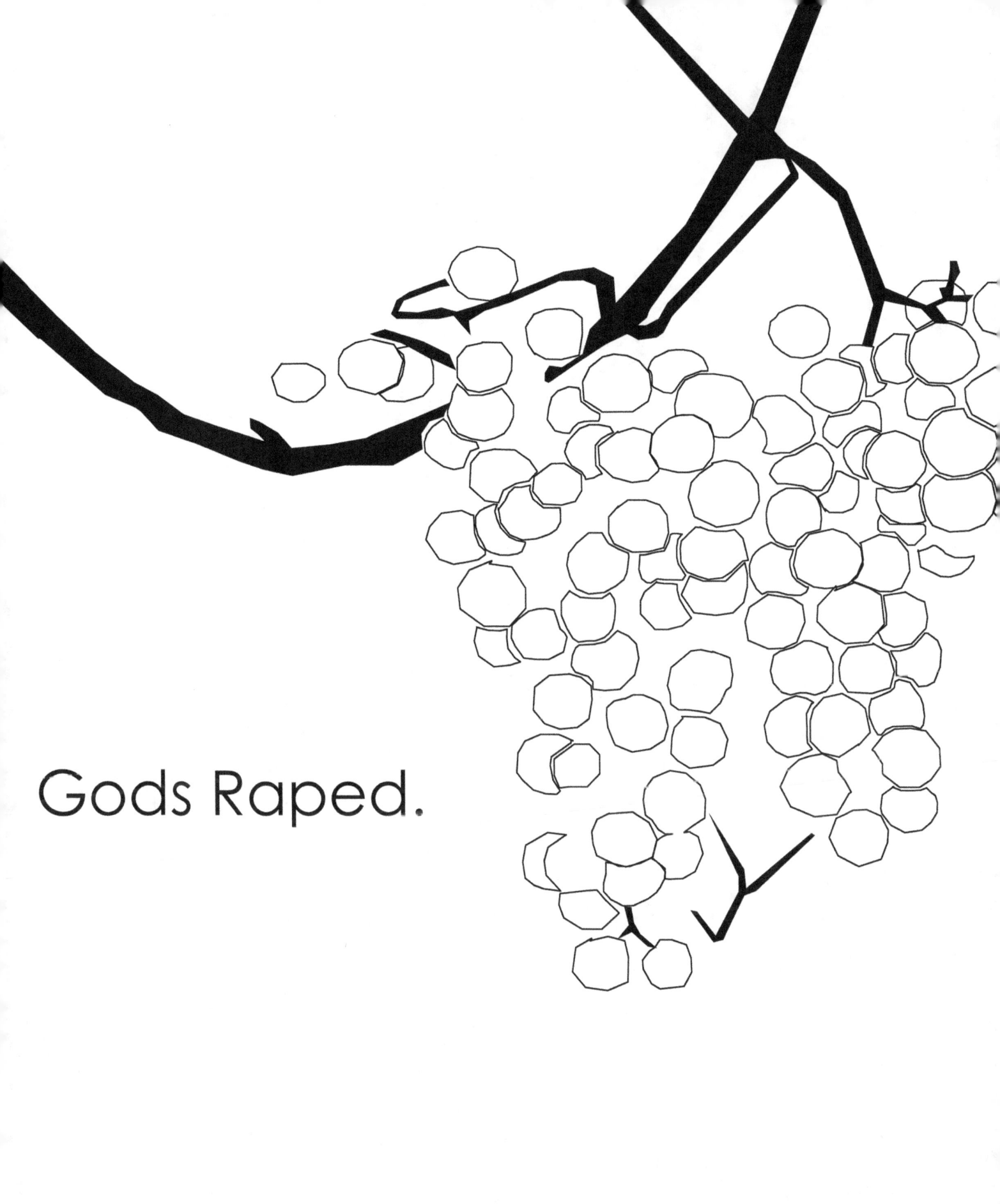

Gods Raped.

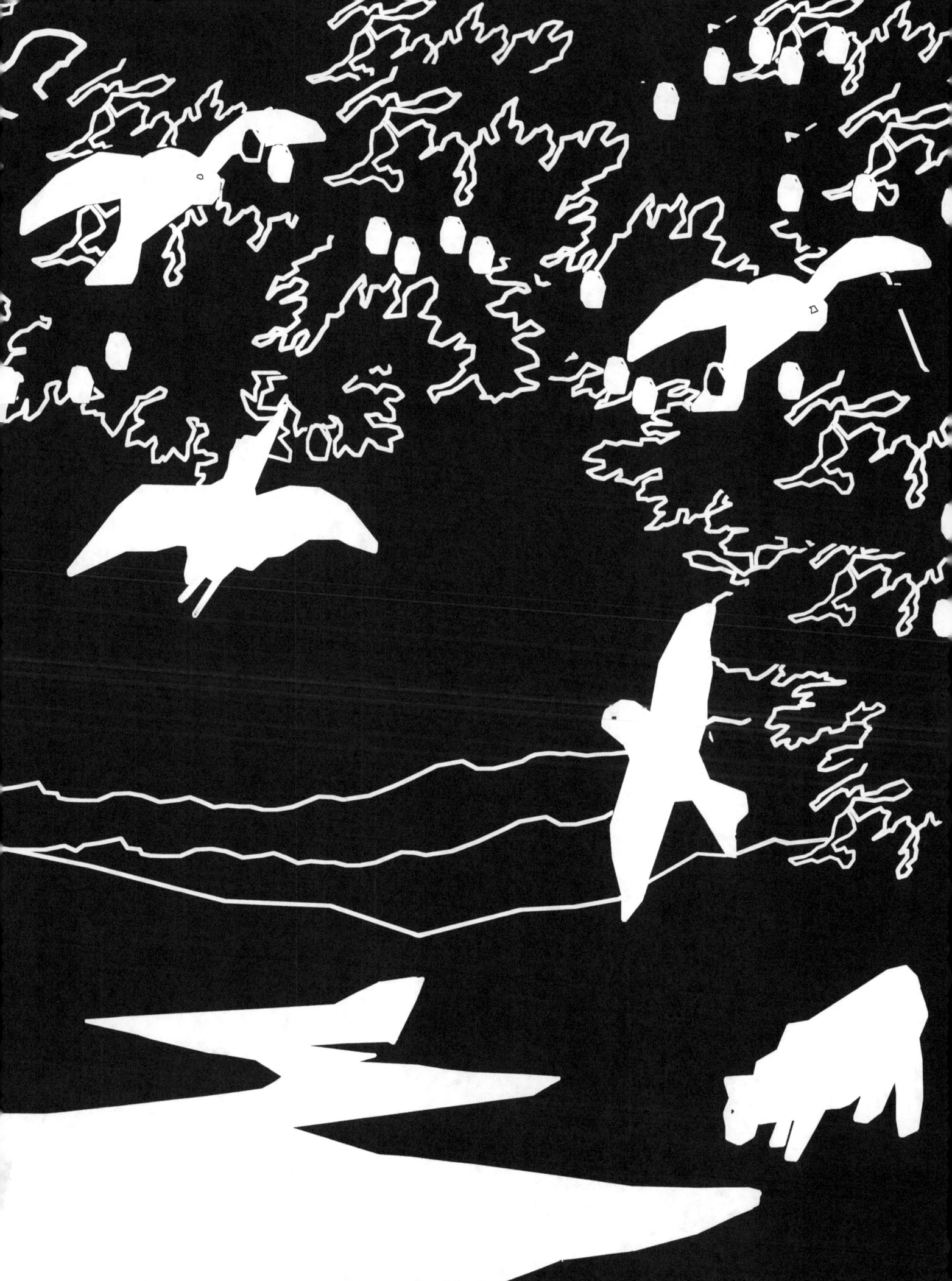

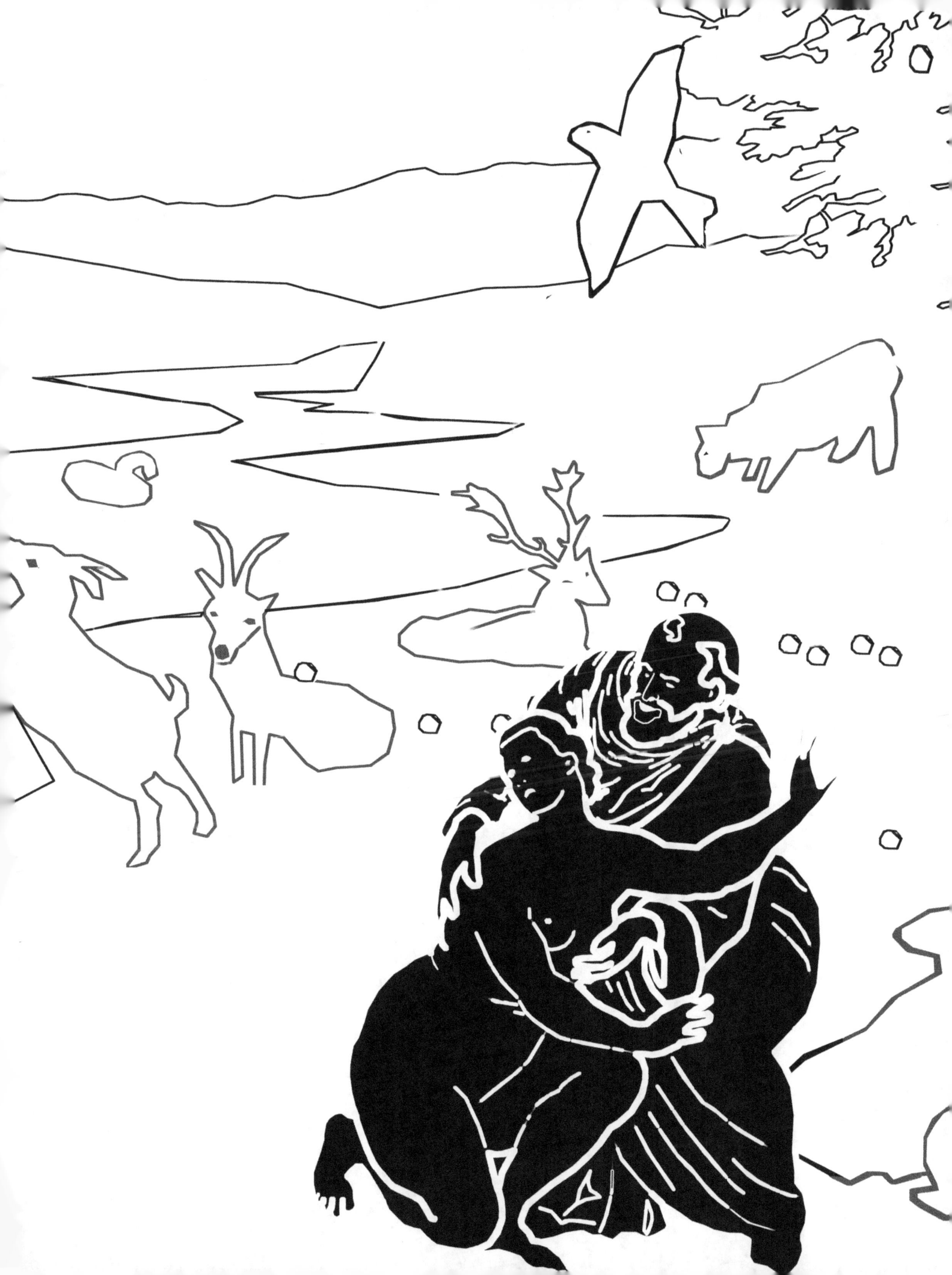

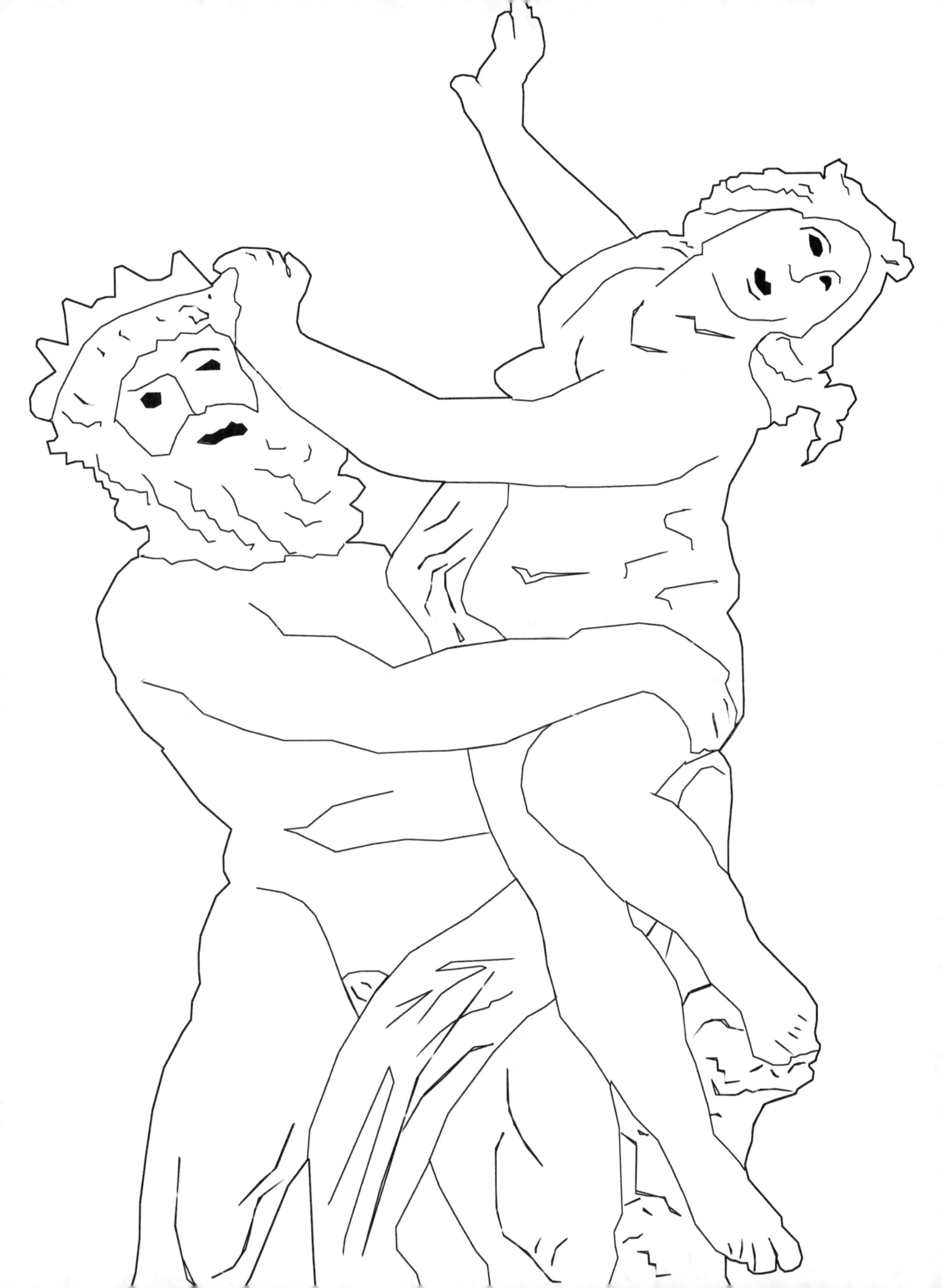

RAPE WAS AS NATURAL
AS THE NATURAL WORLD.

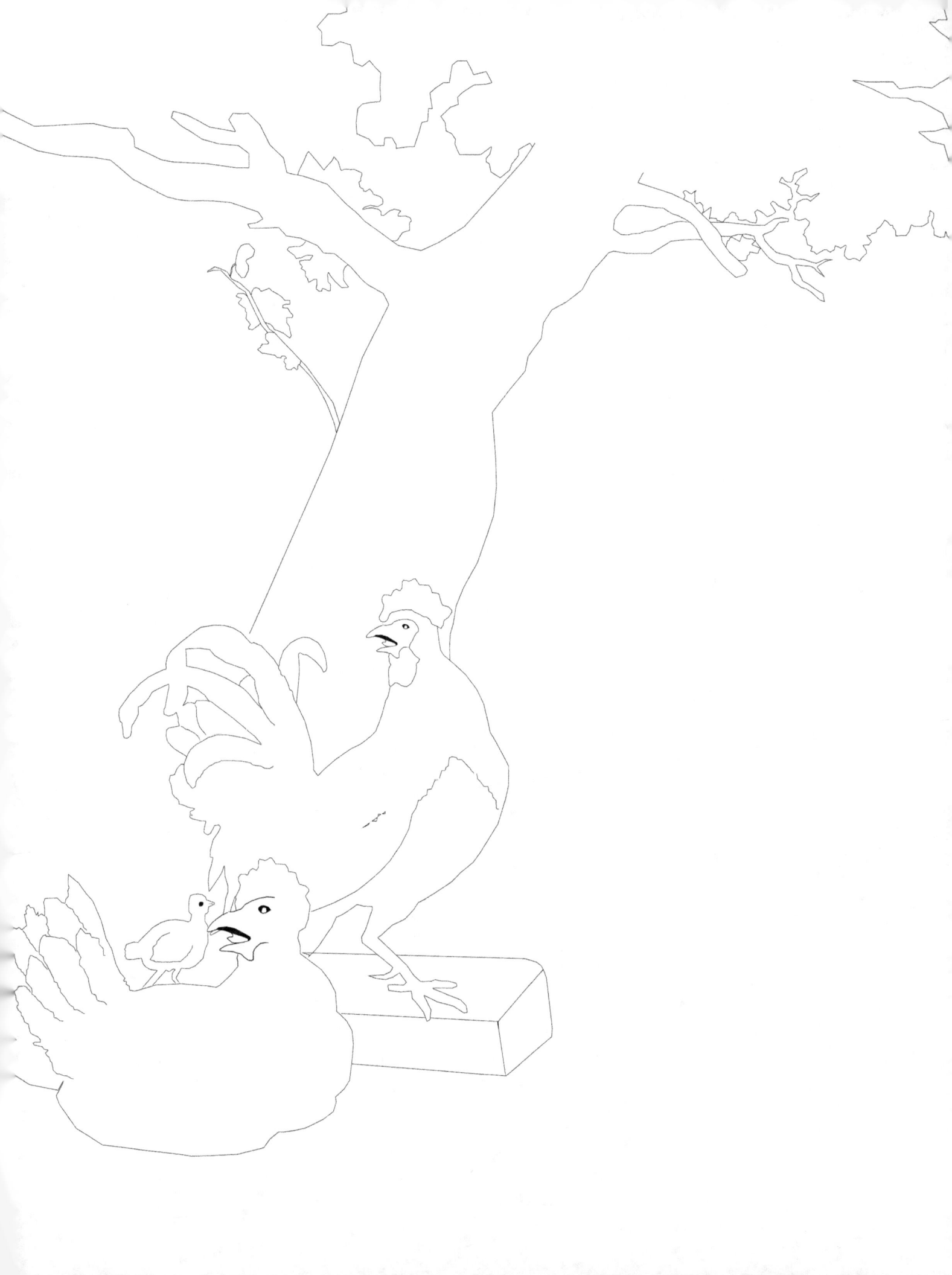

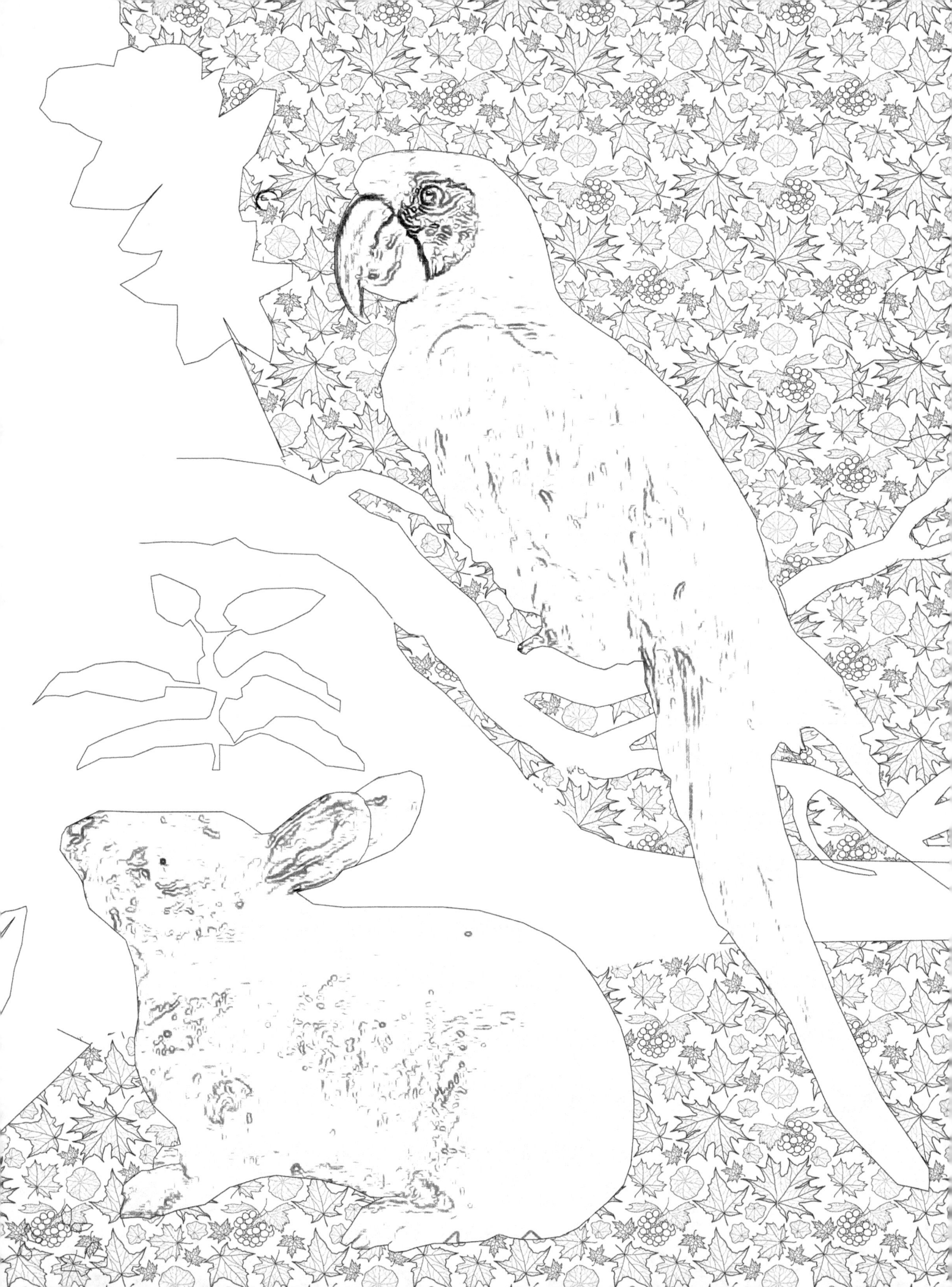

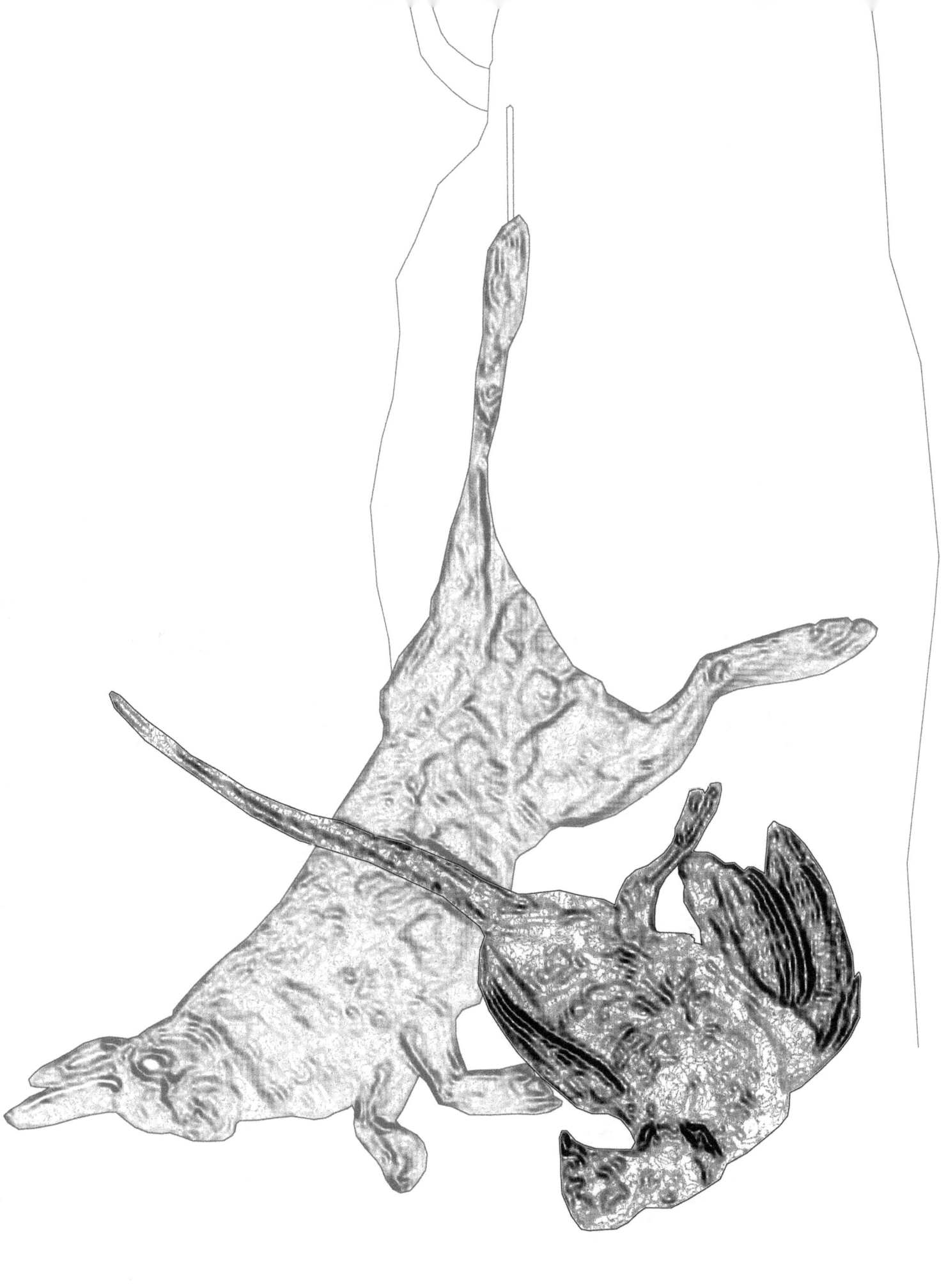

WOMEN DID NOT OWN THEIR BODIES.

THERE WAS NOTHING TO CHOOSE.

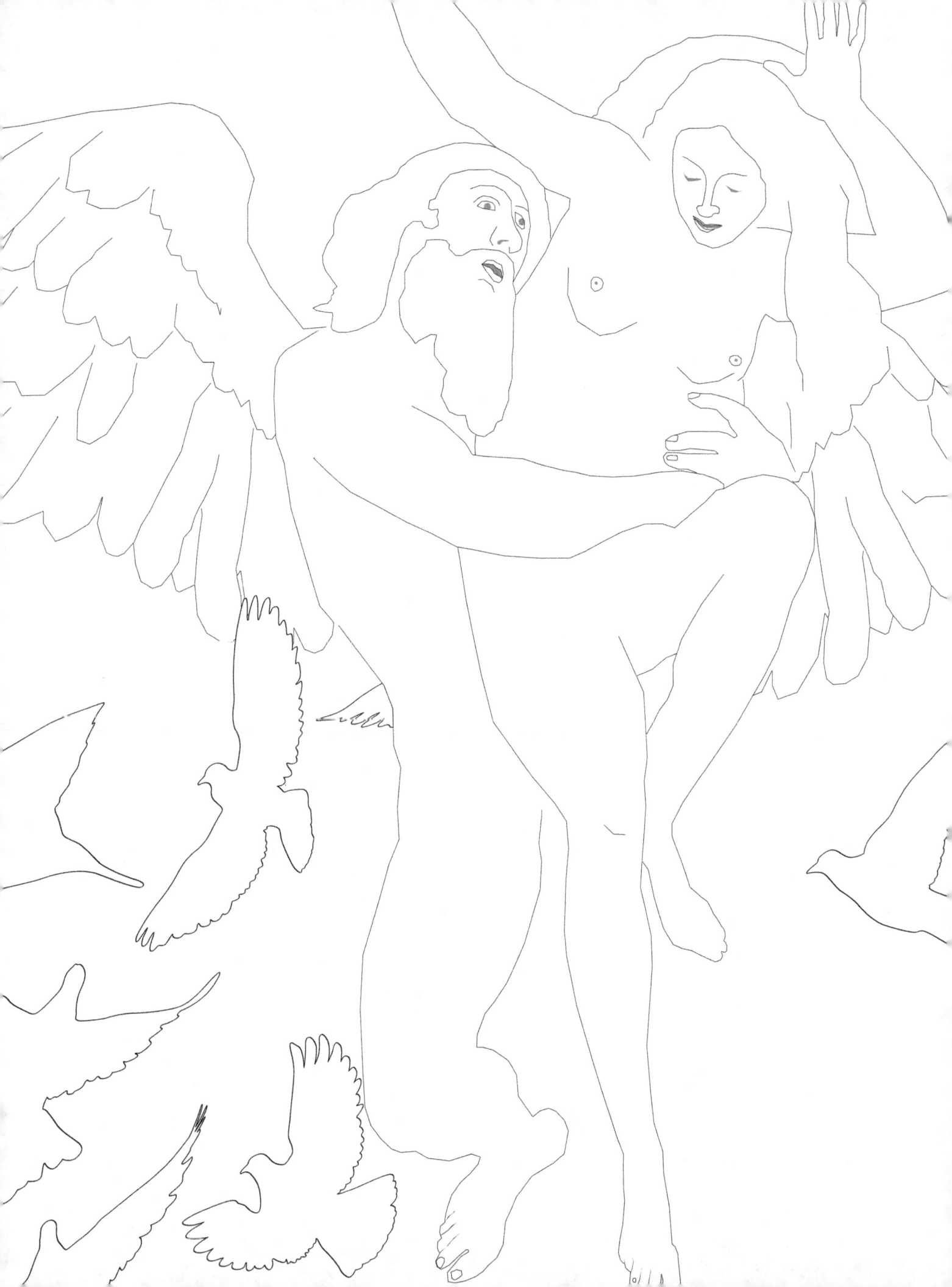

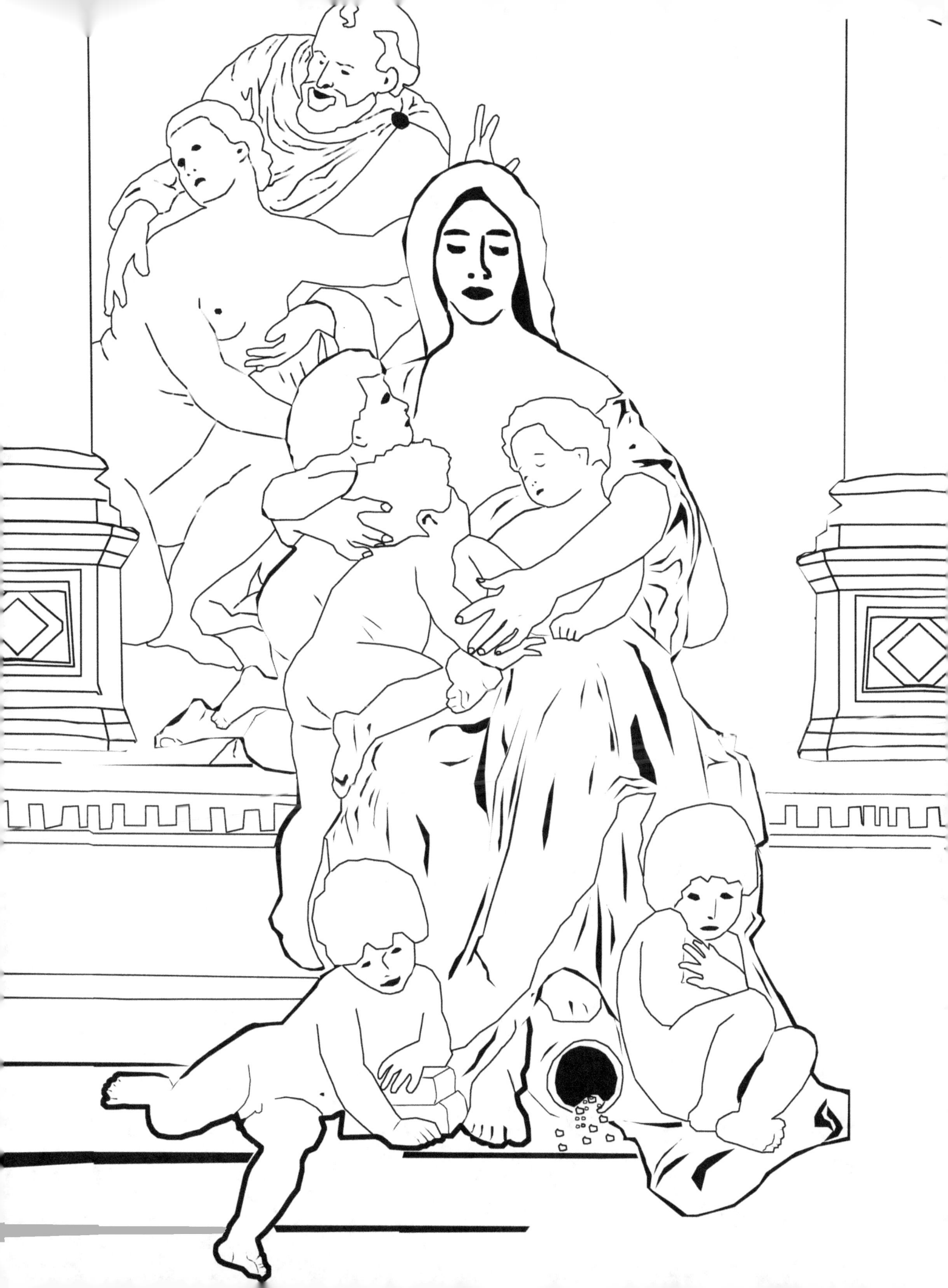

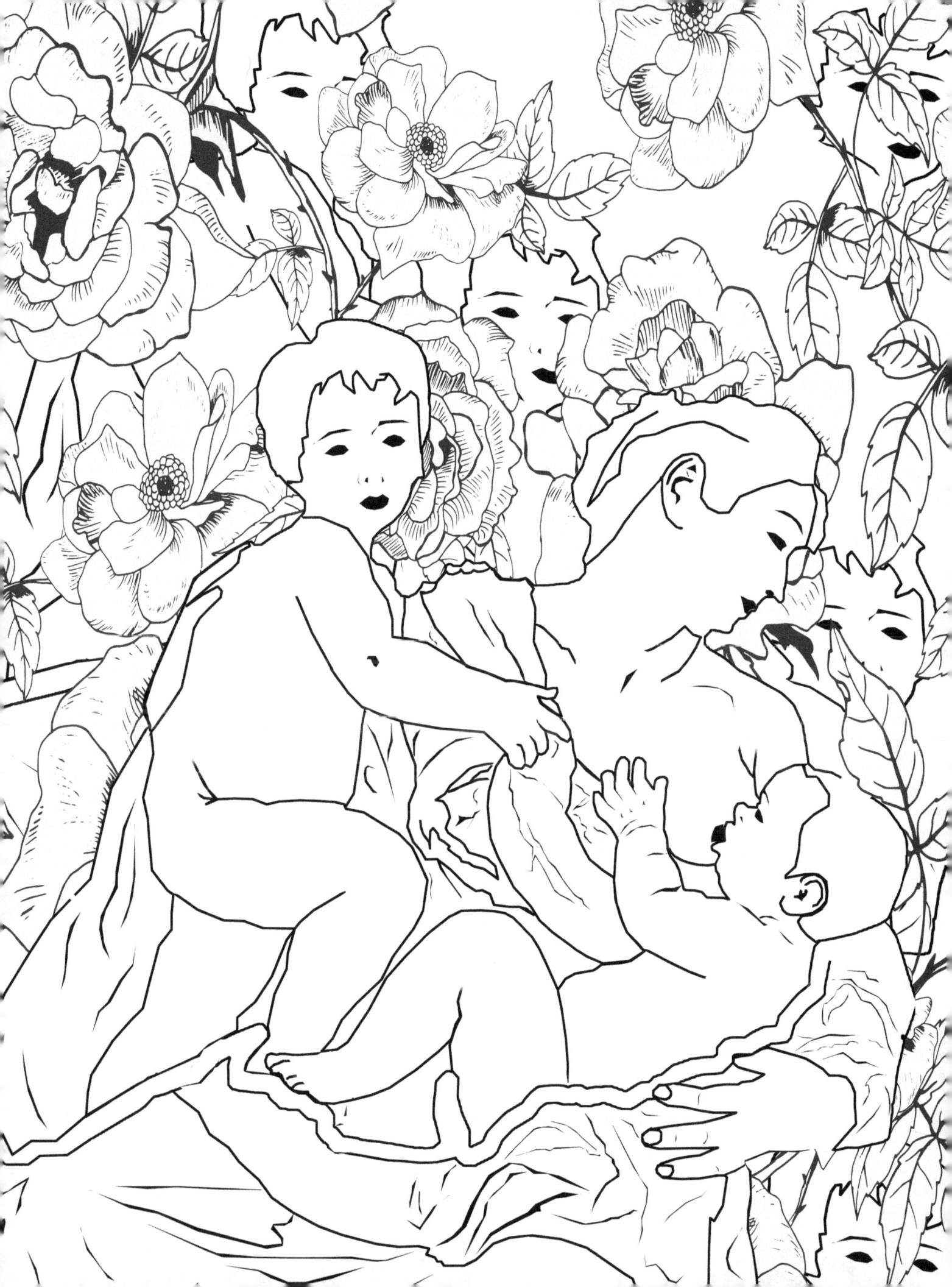

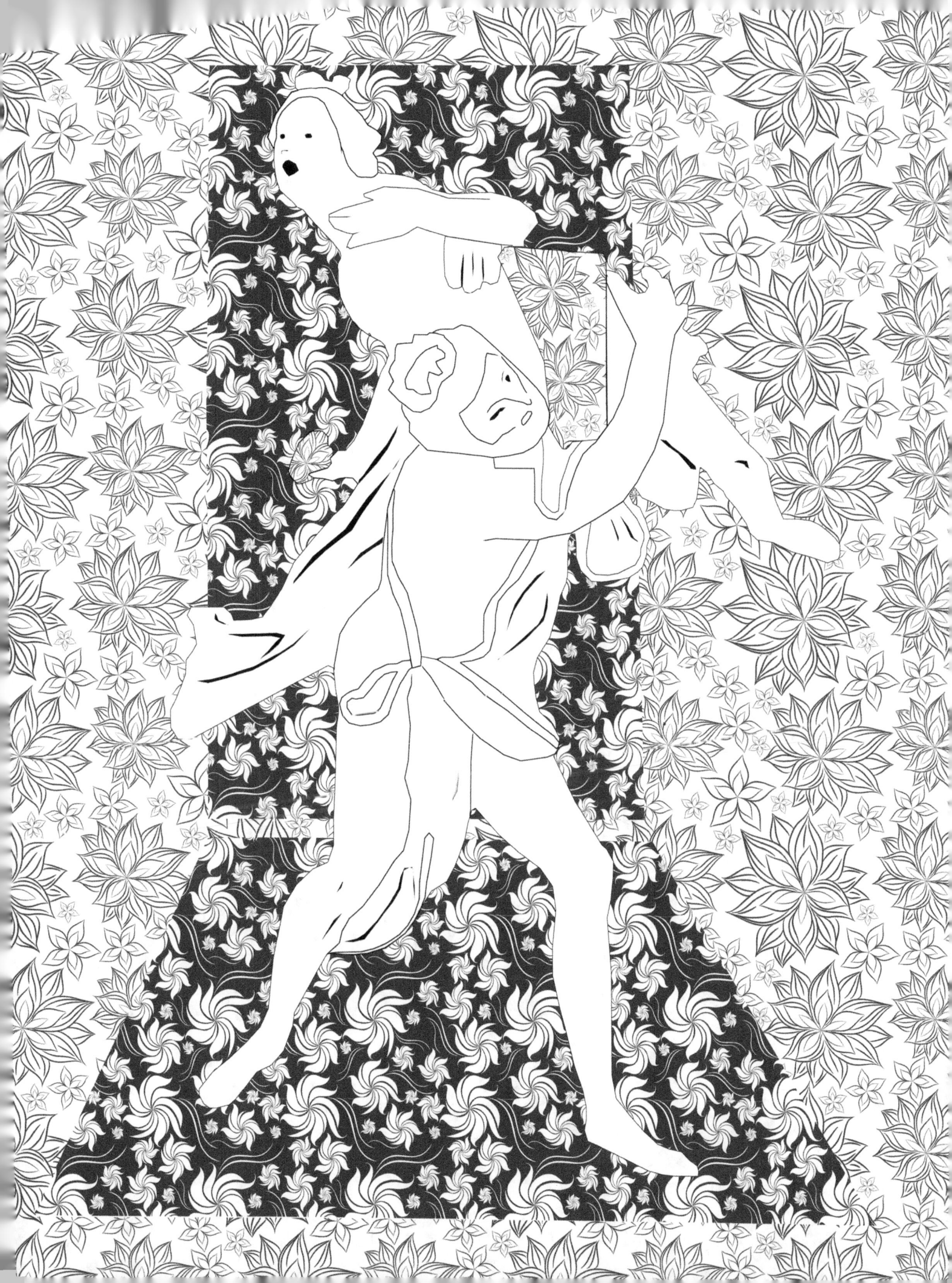

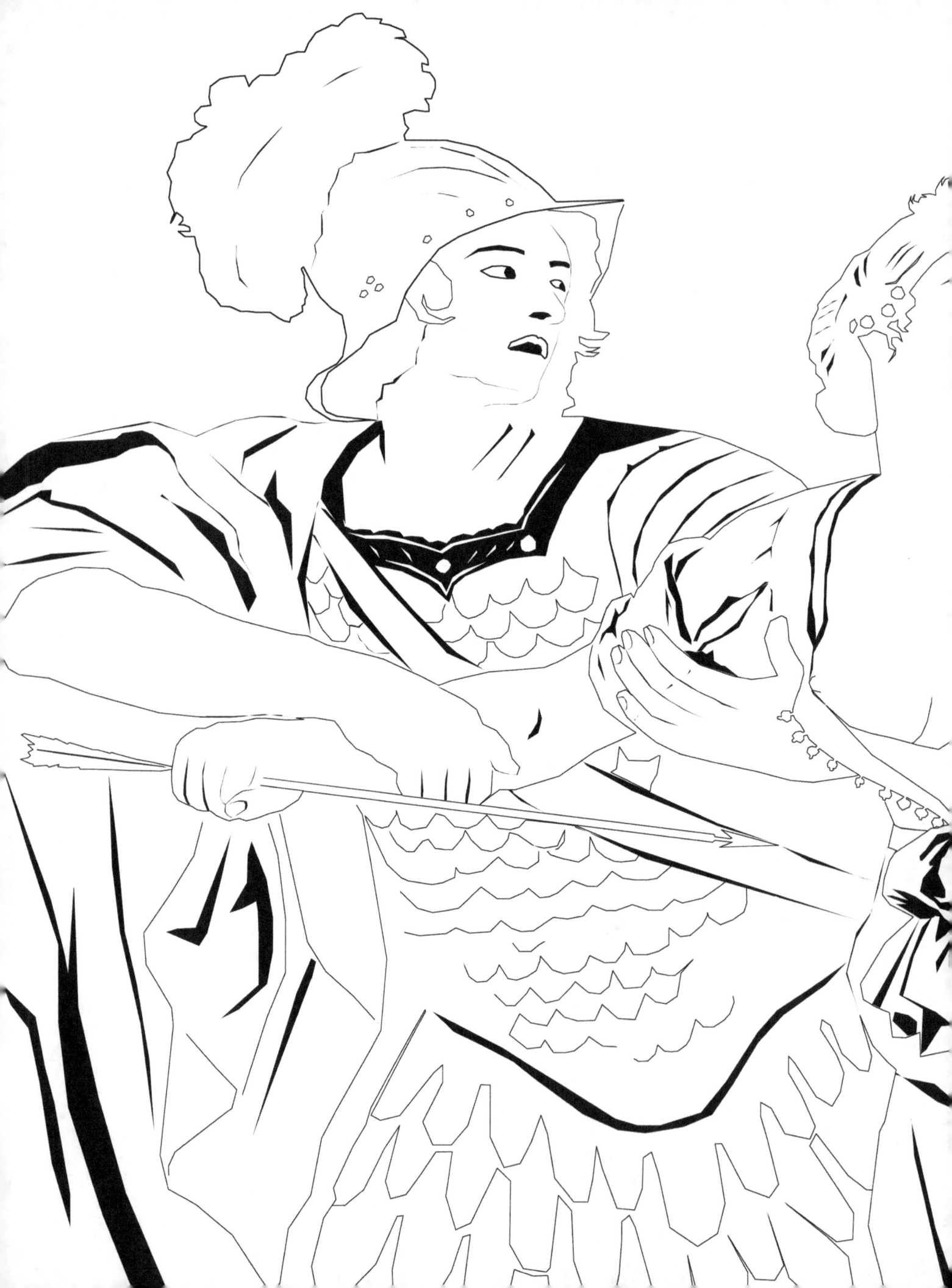

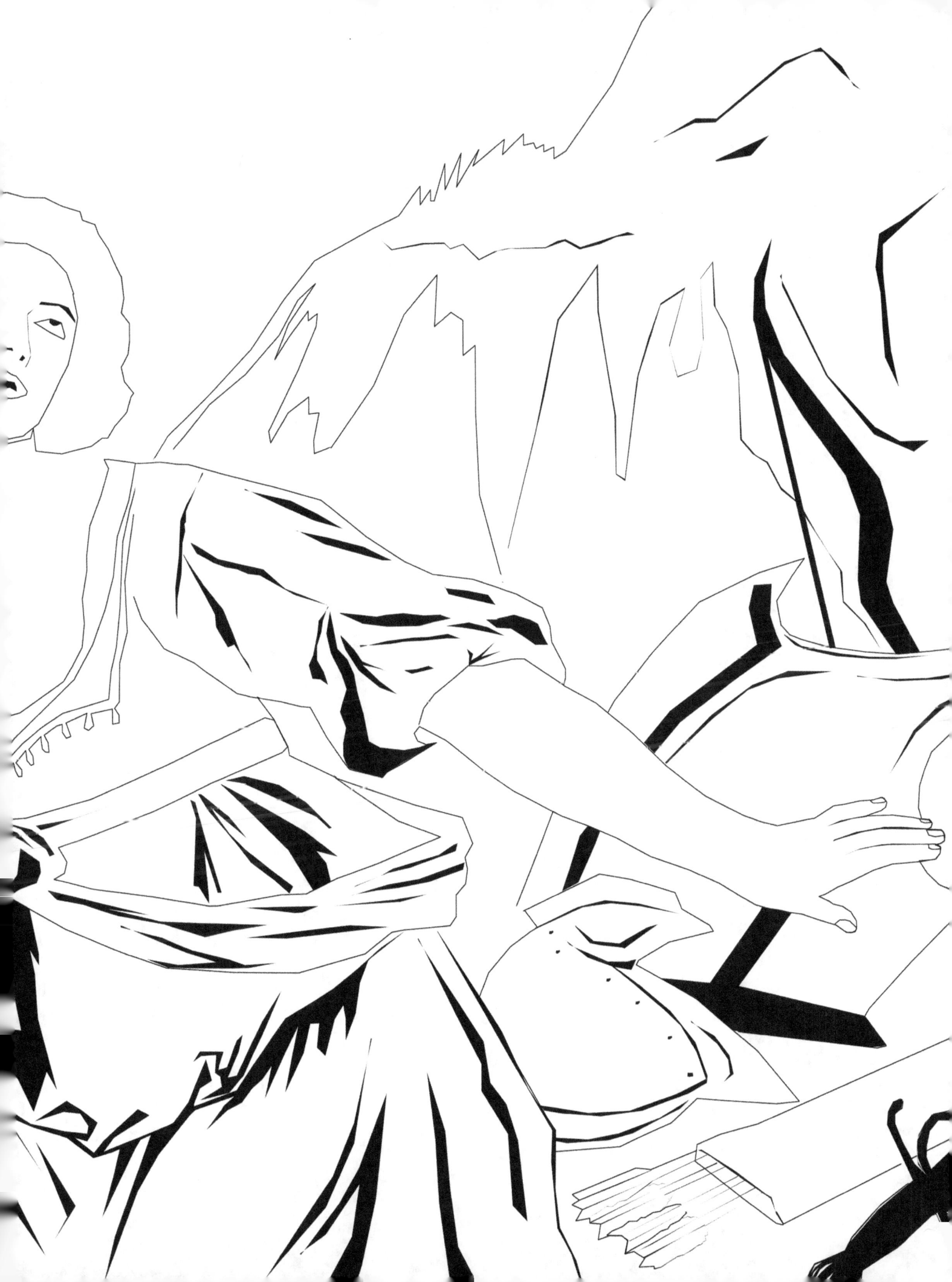

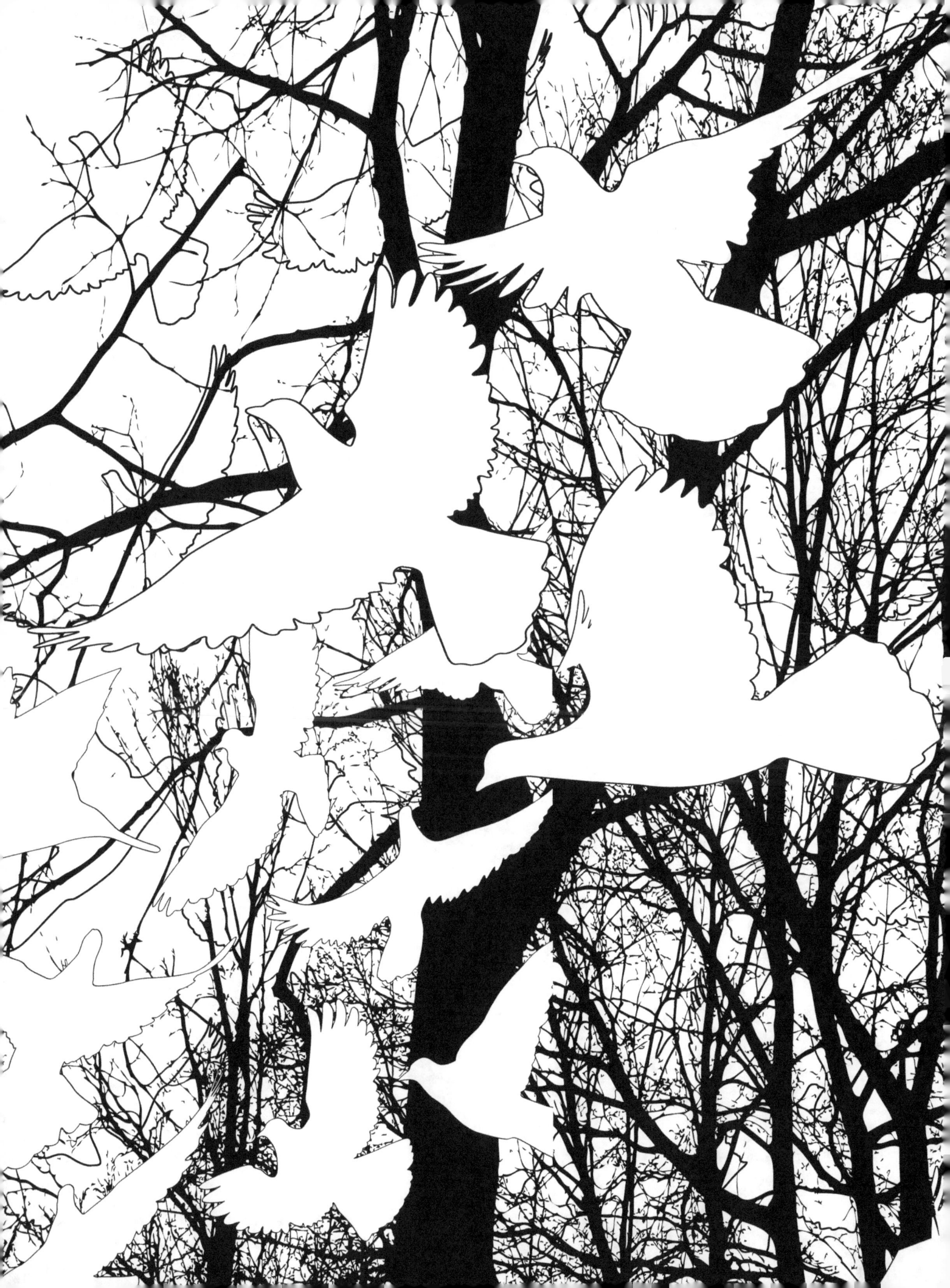

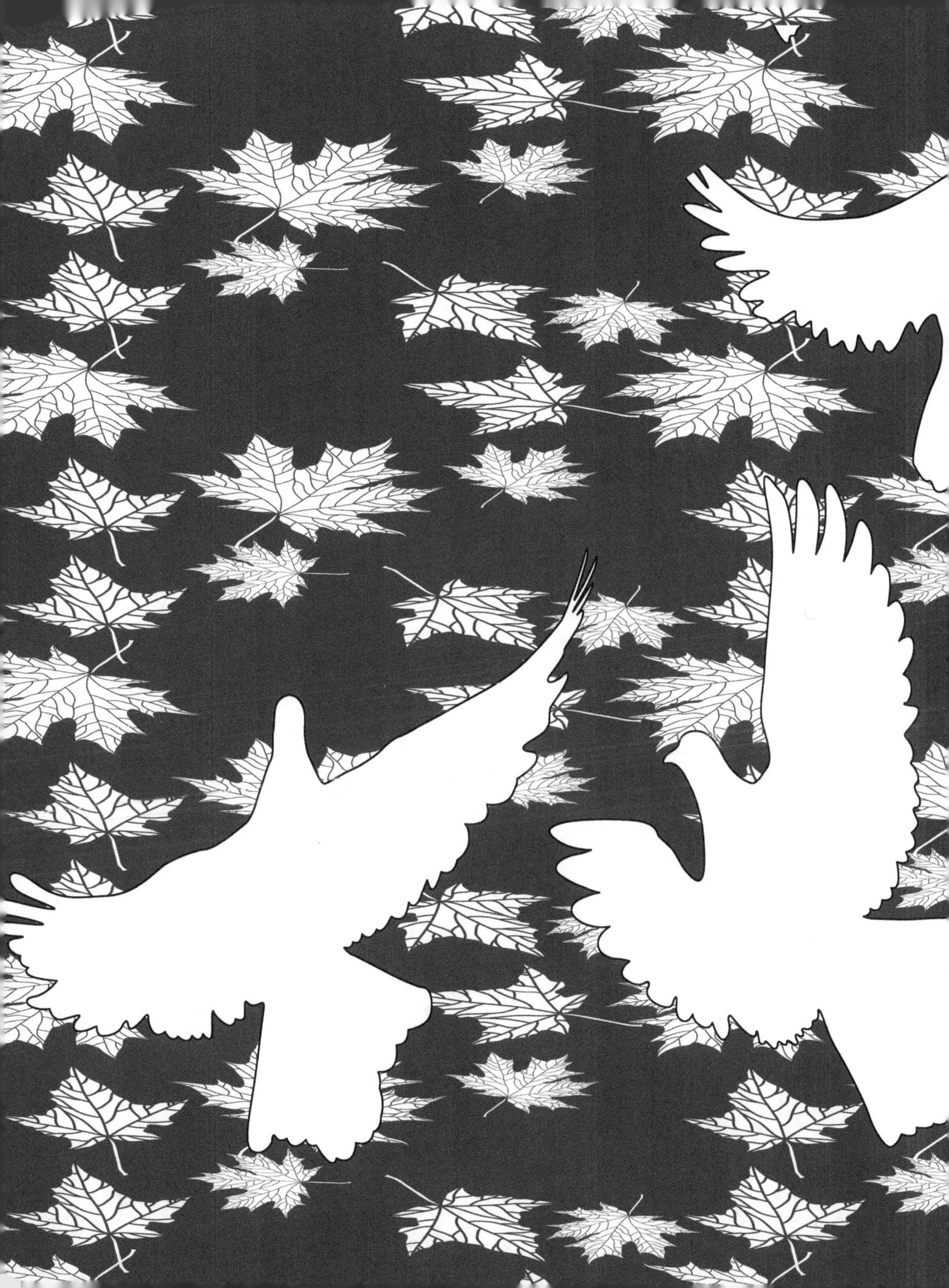

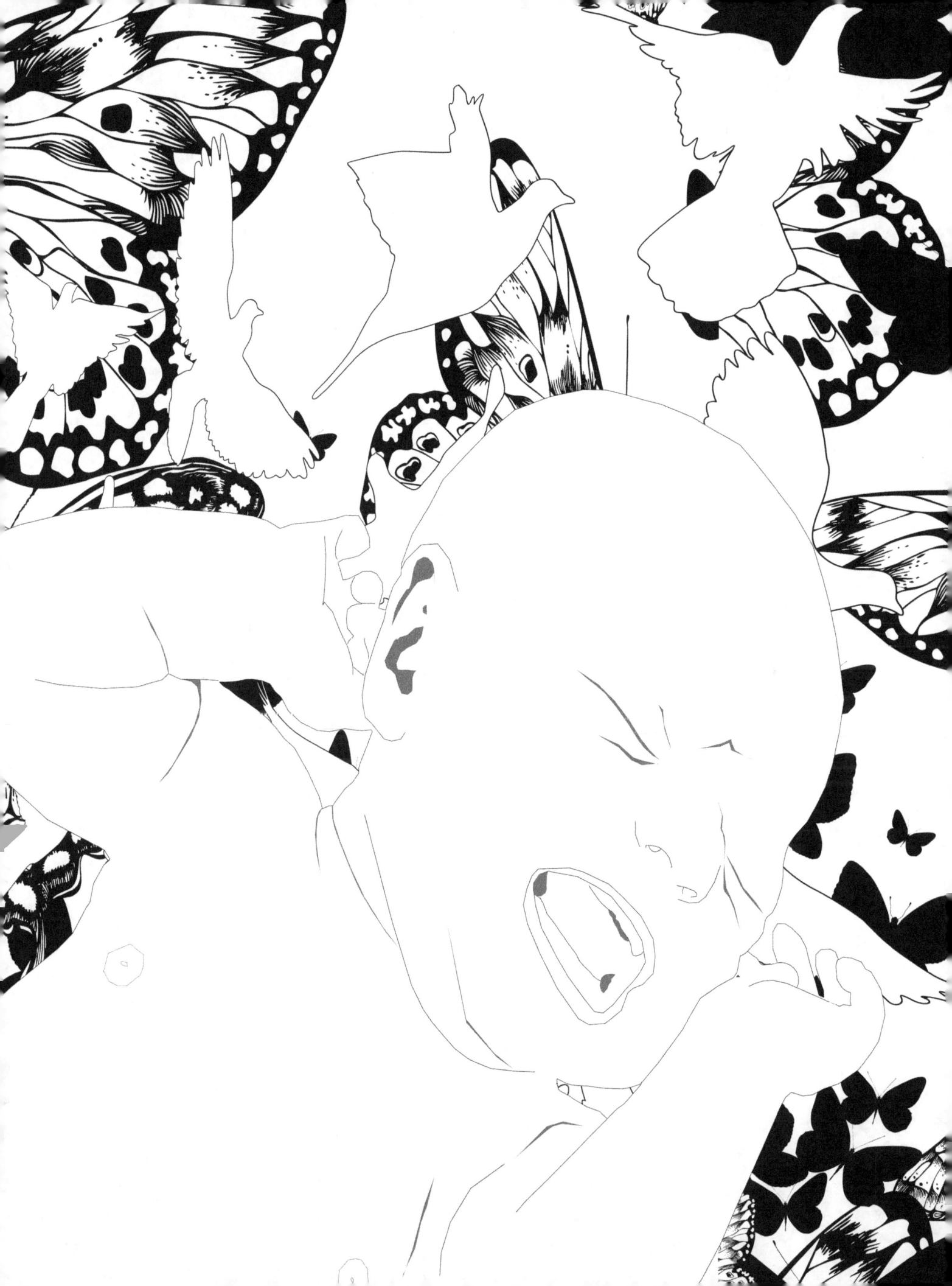

**WOMEN'S ECSTASY WAS
FOR THE LOVE OF GOD ALONE.**

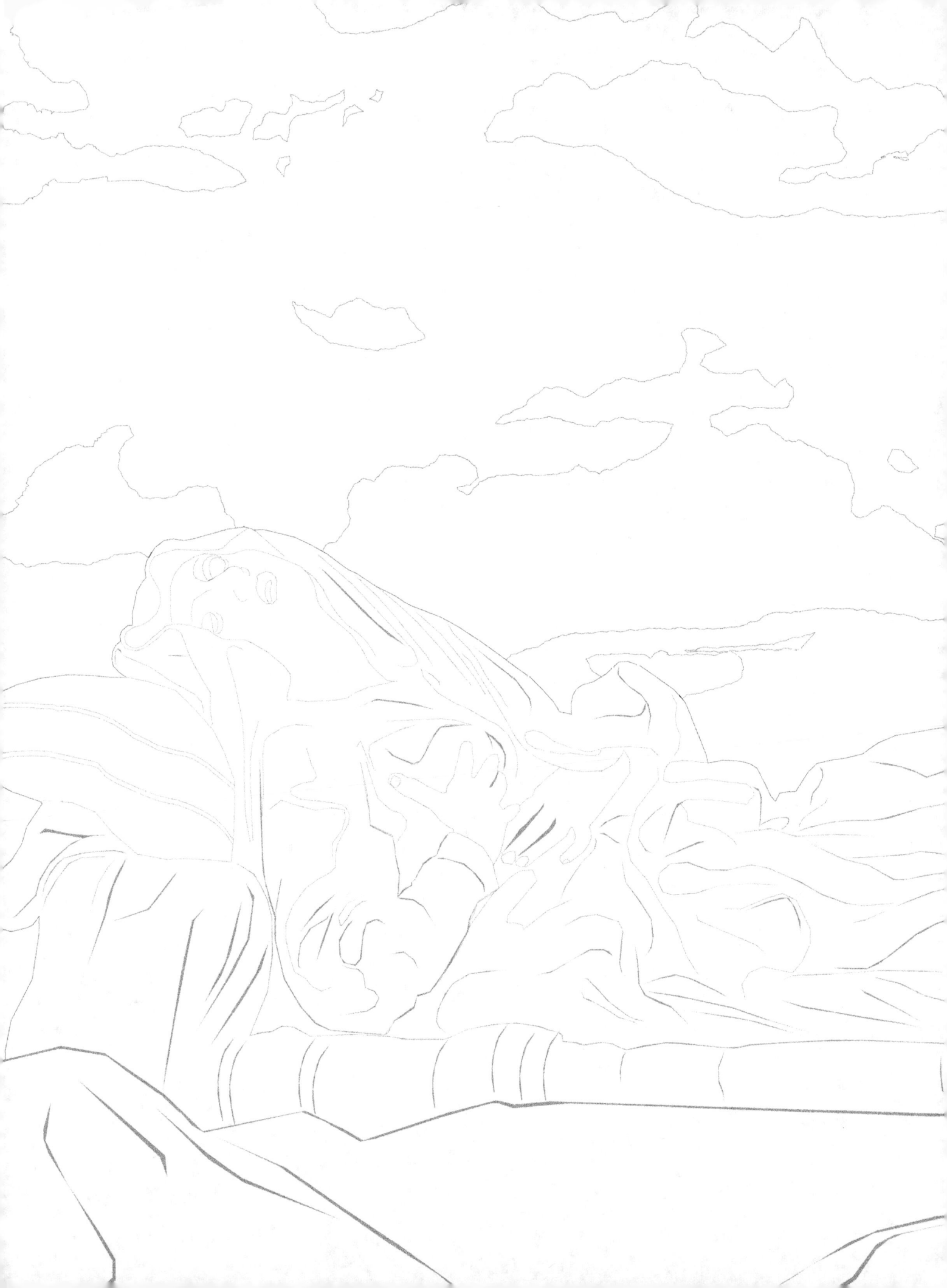

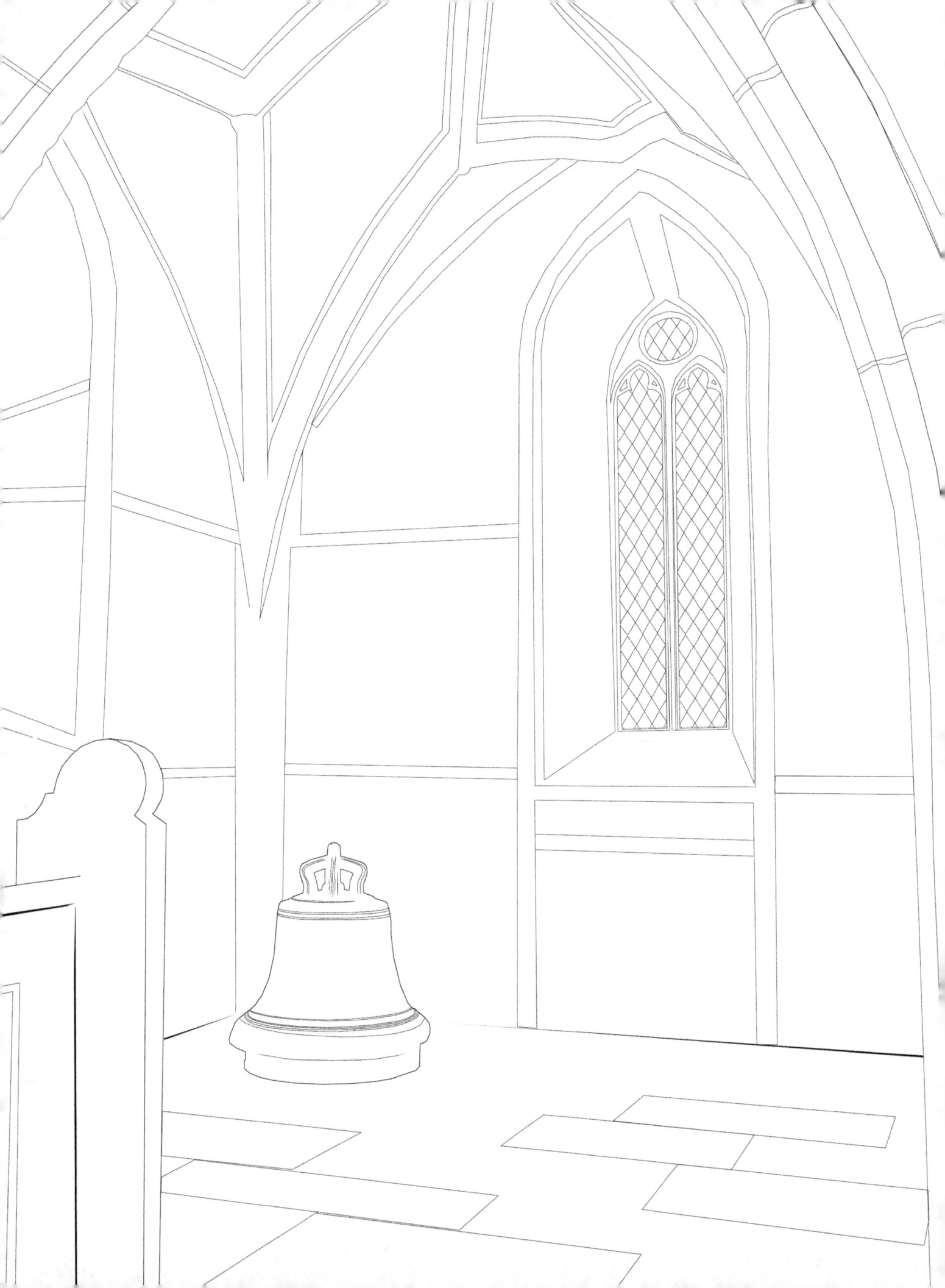

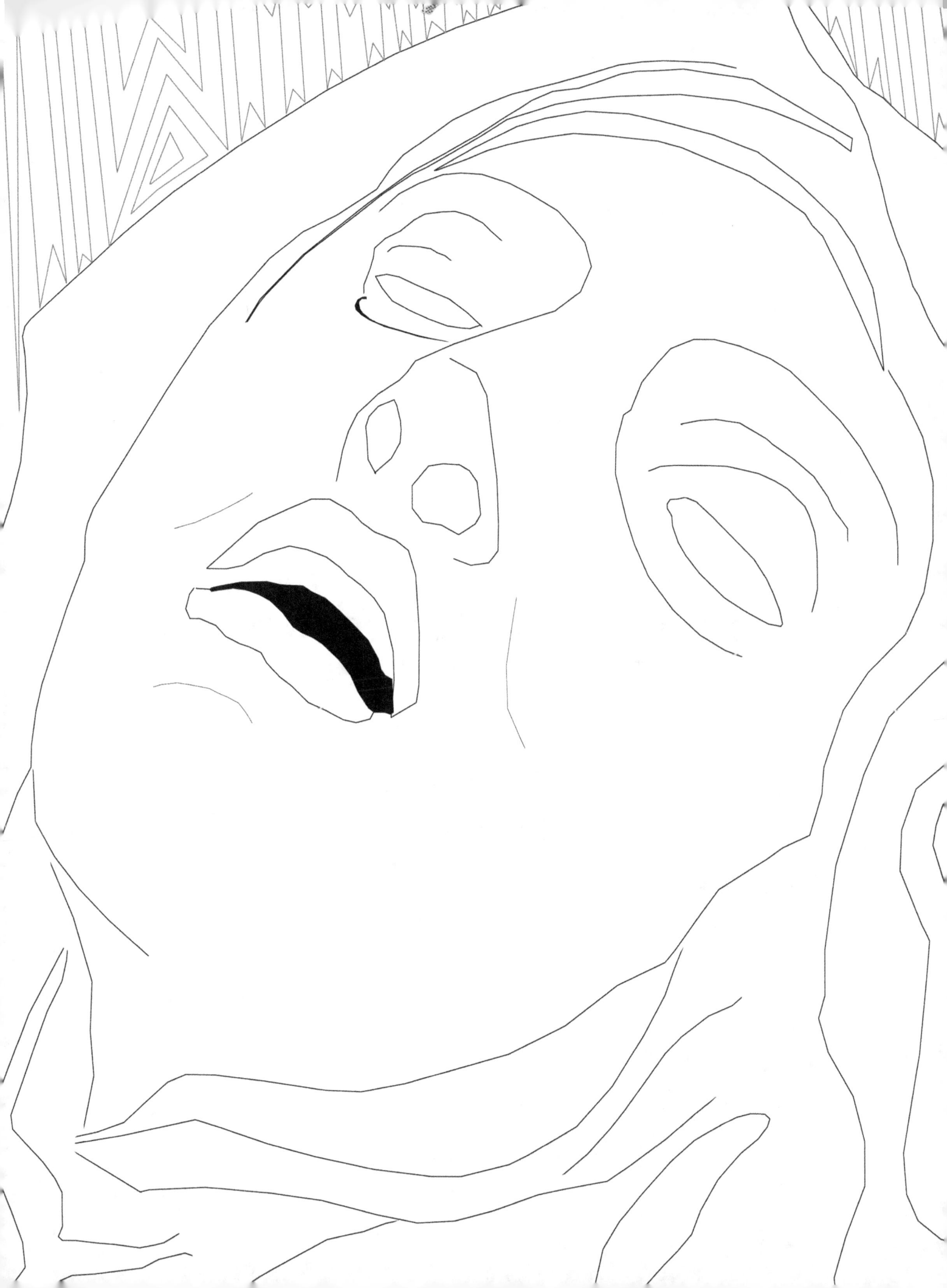

AND WOMEN WERE PUNISHED
FOR THEIR RAPES.

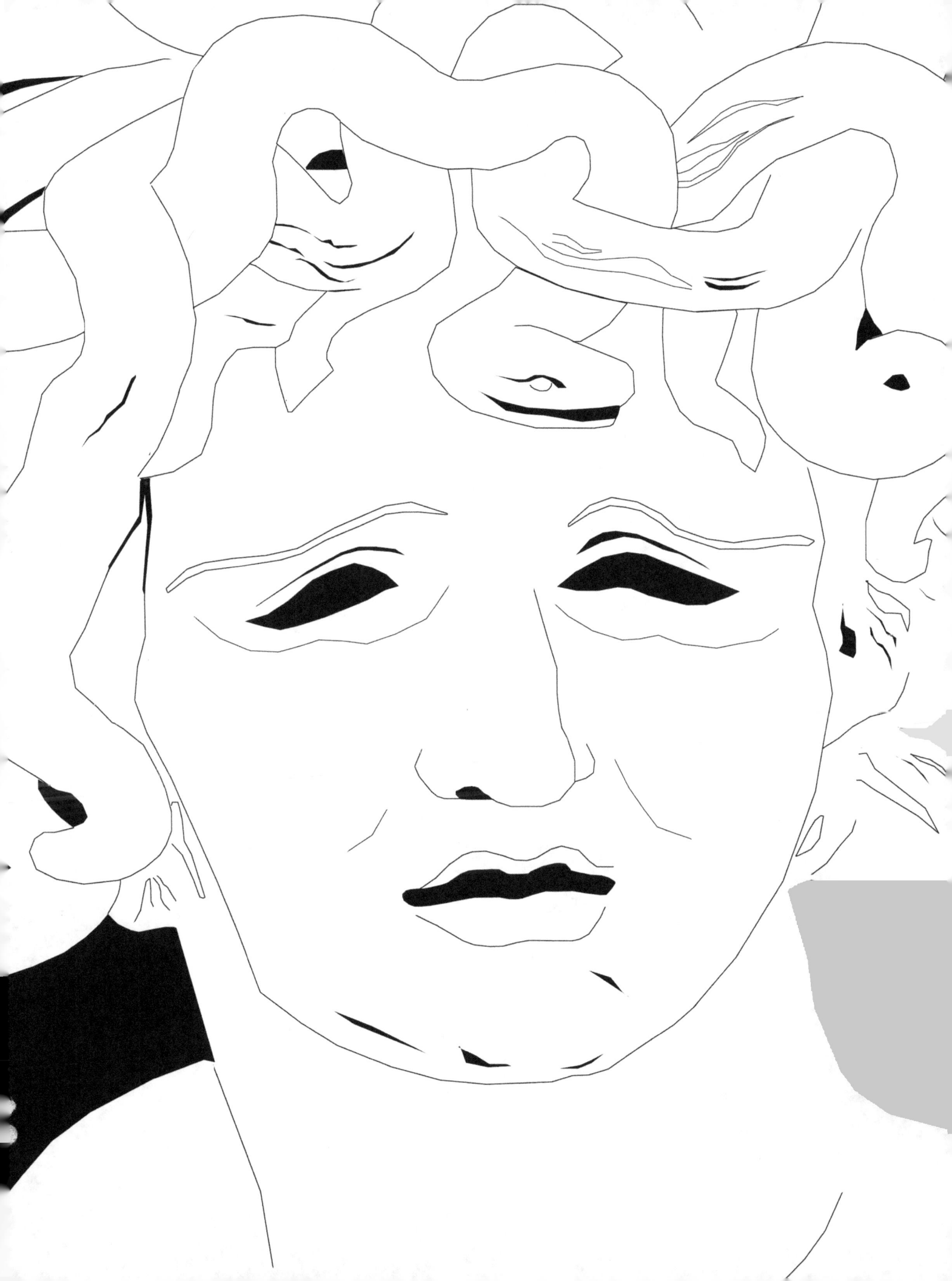

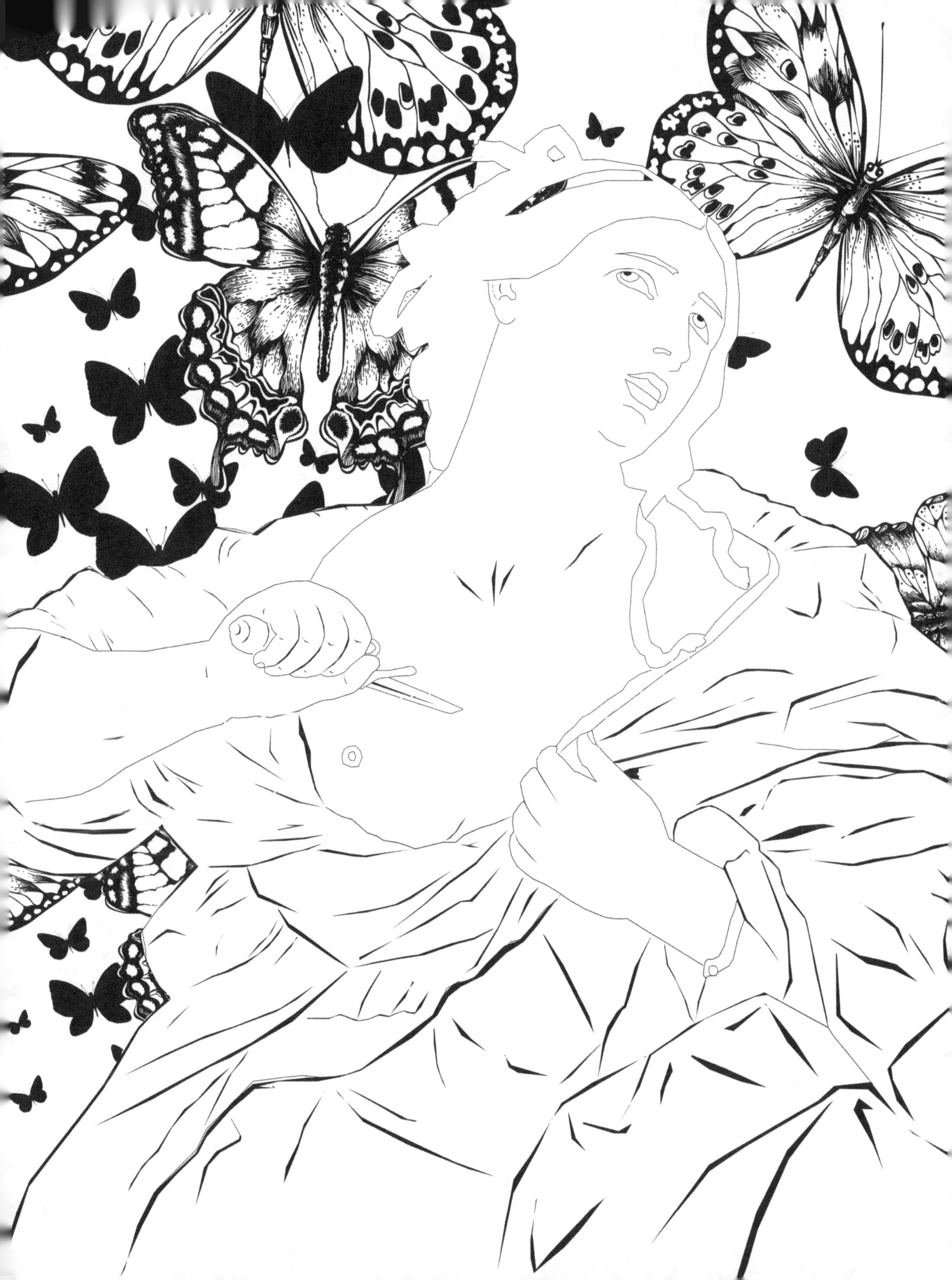

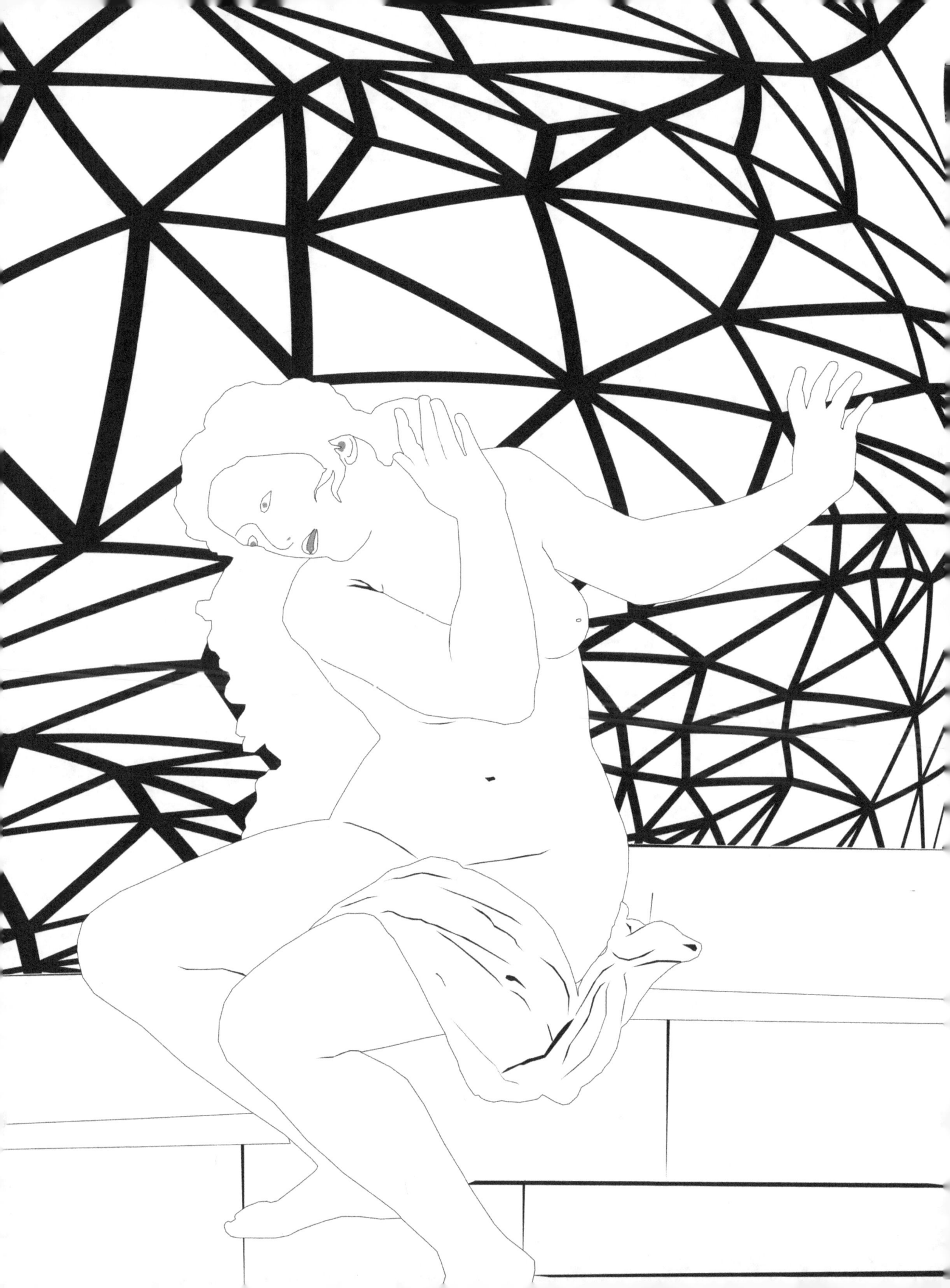

NO ONE MOURNED.

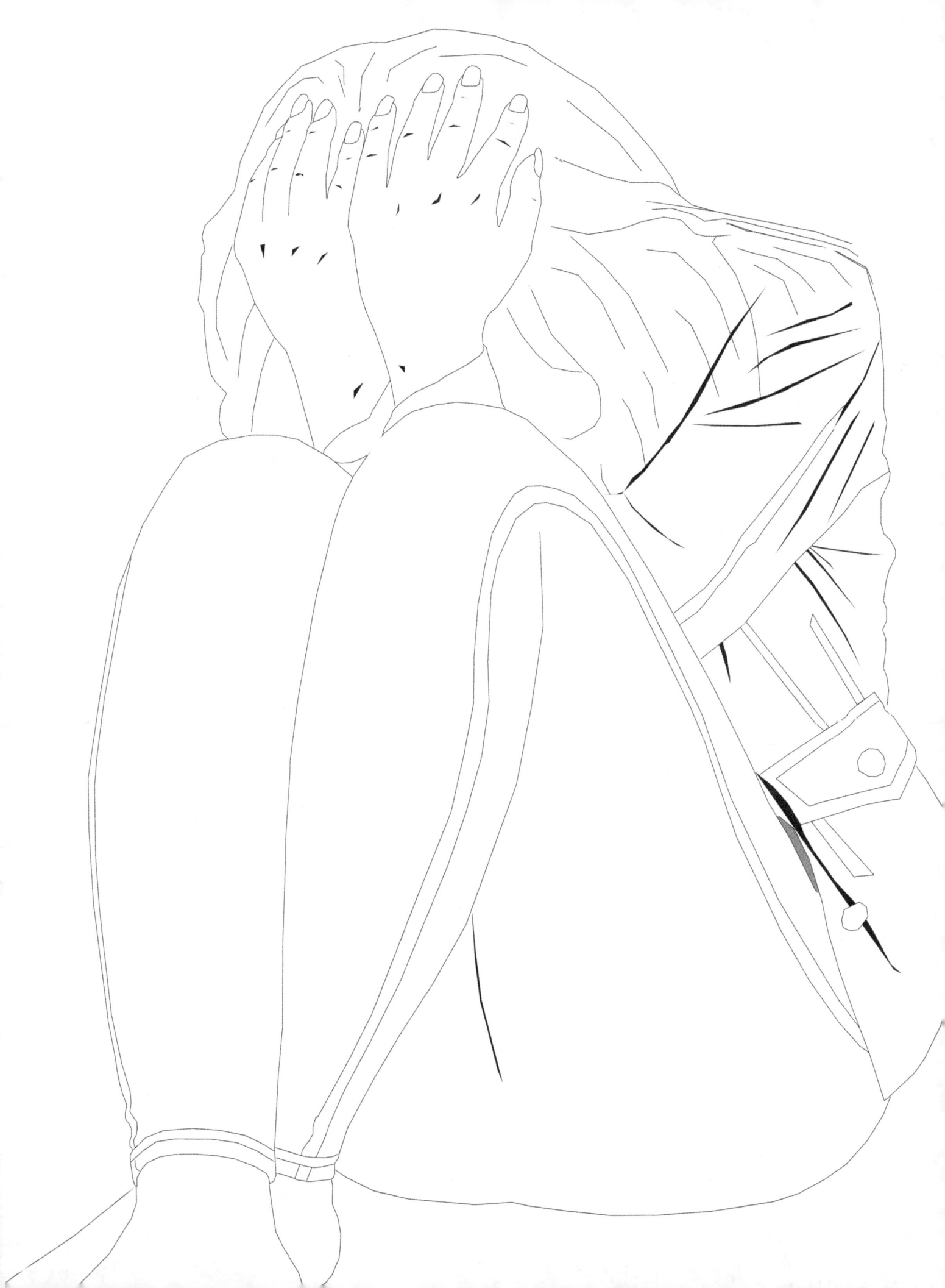

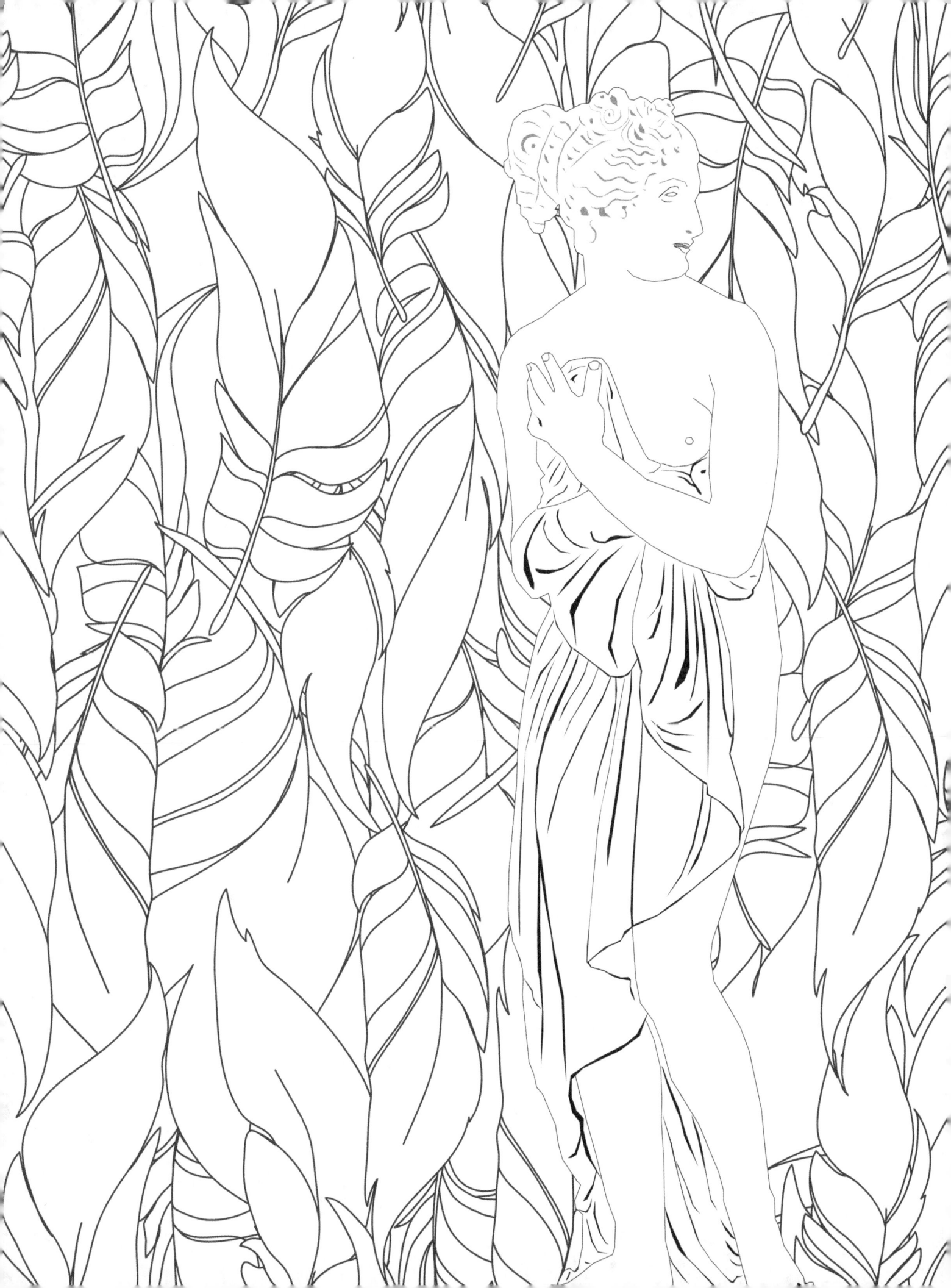

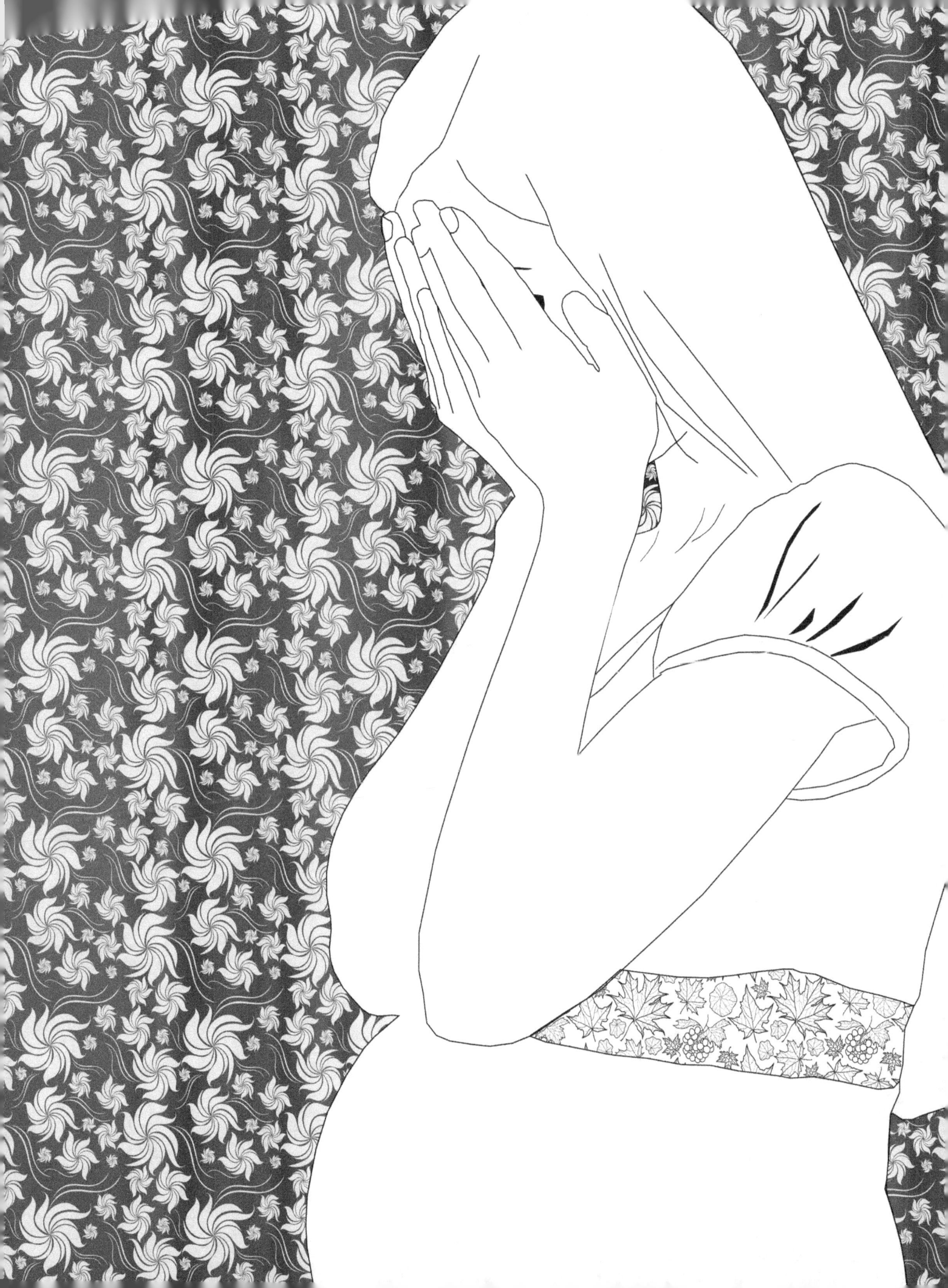

# THE CULTURE HAS CHANGED.

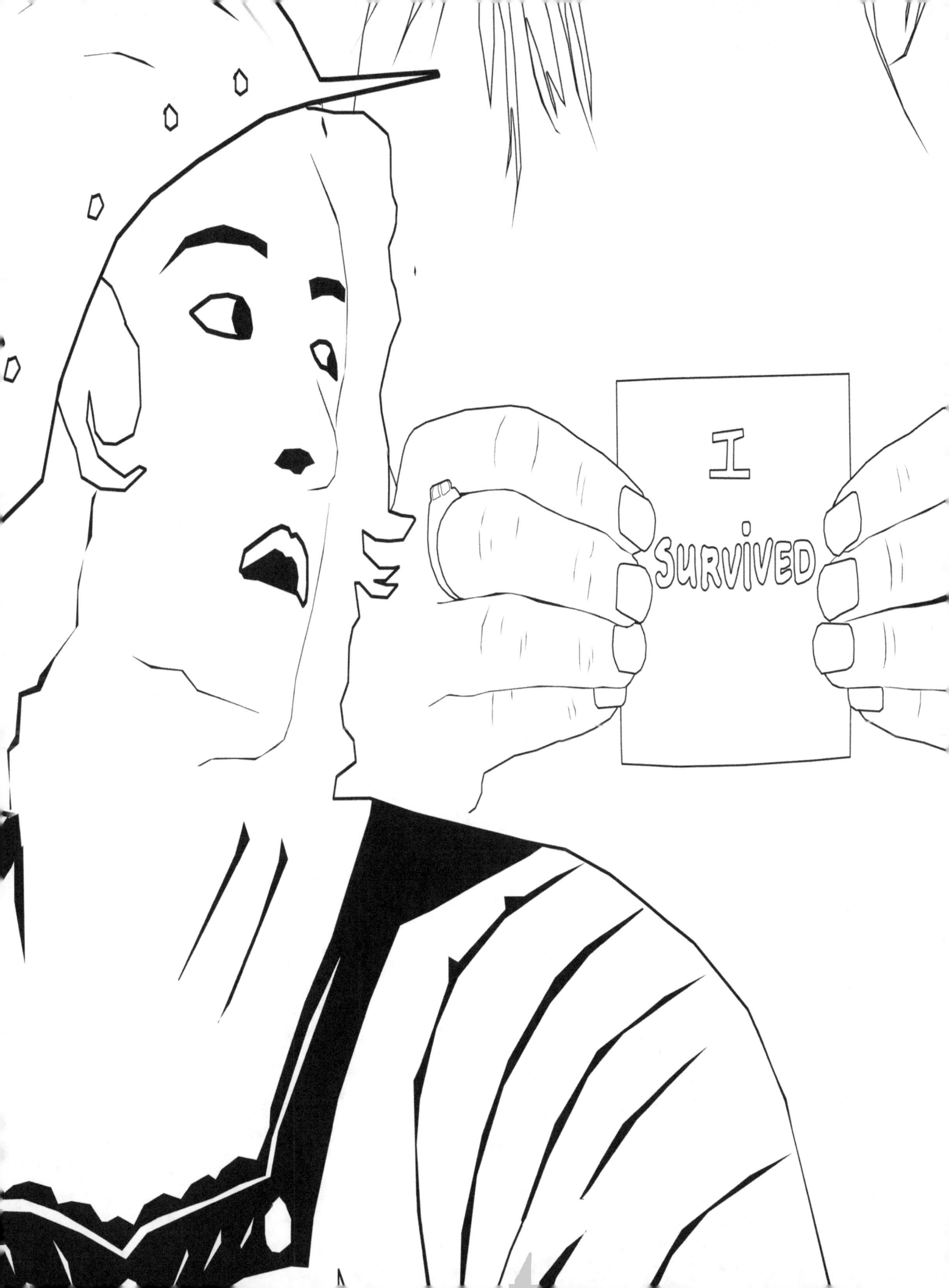

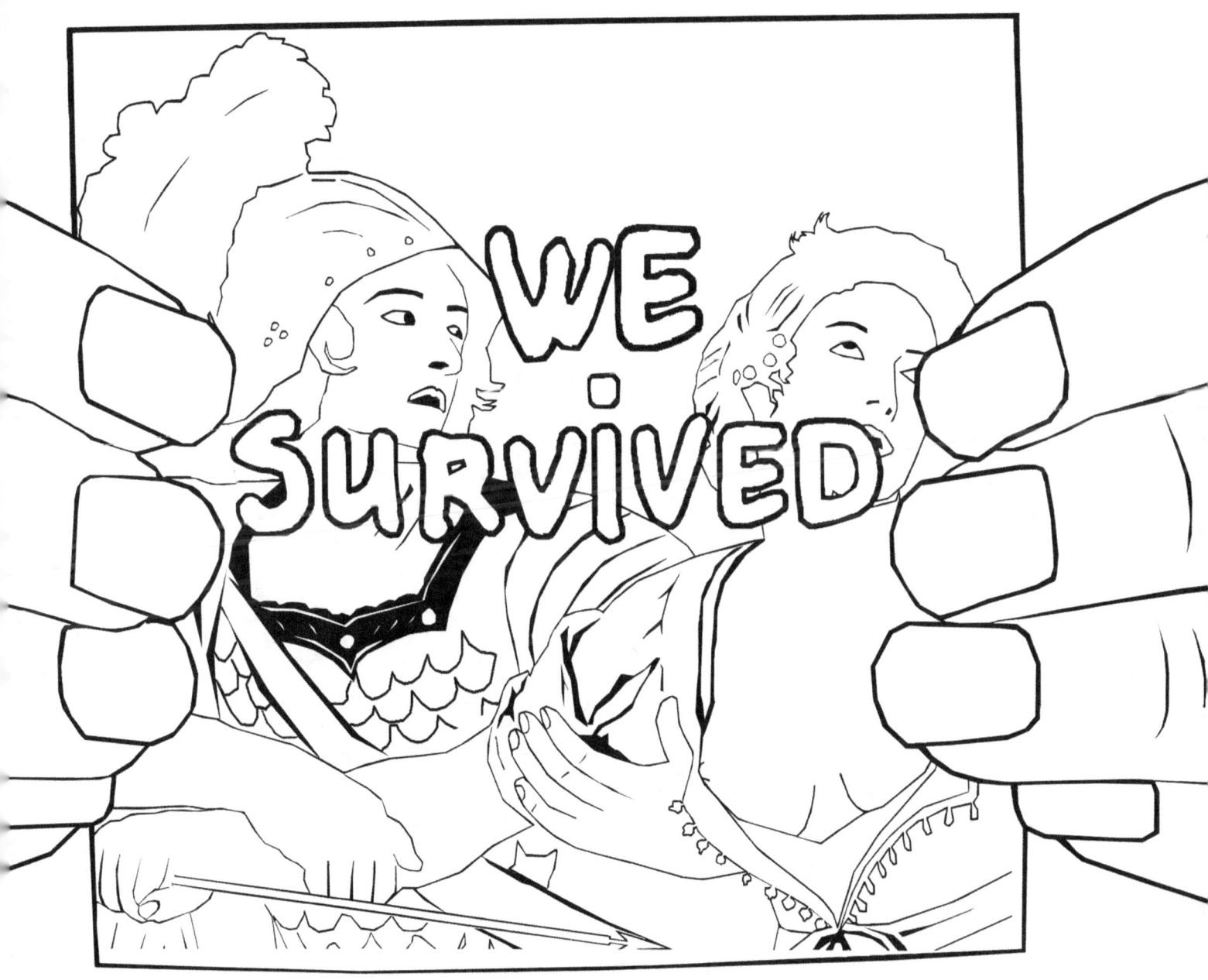

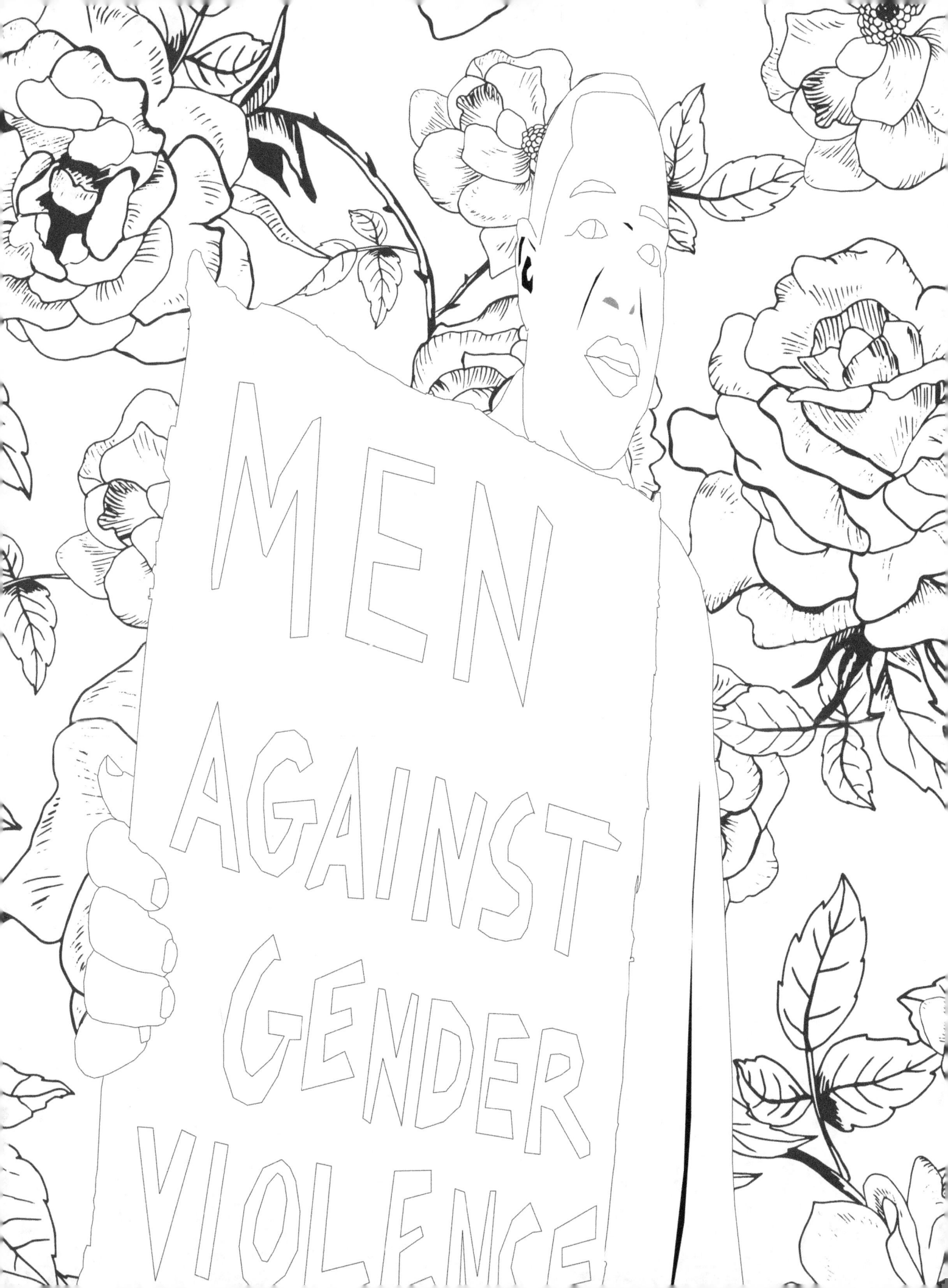

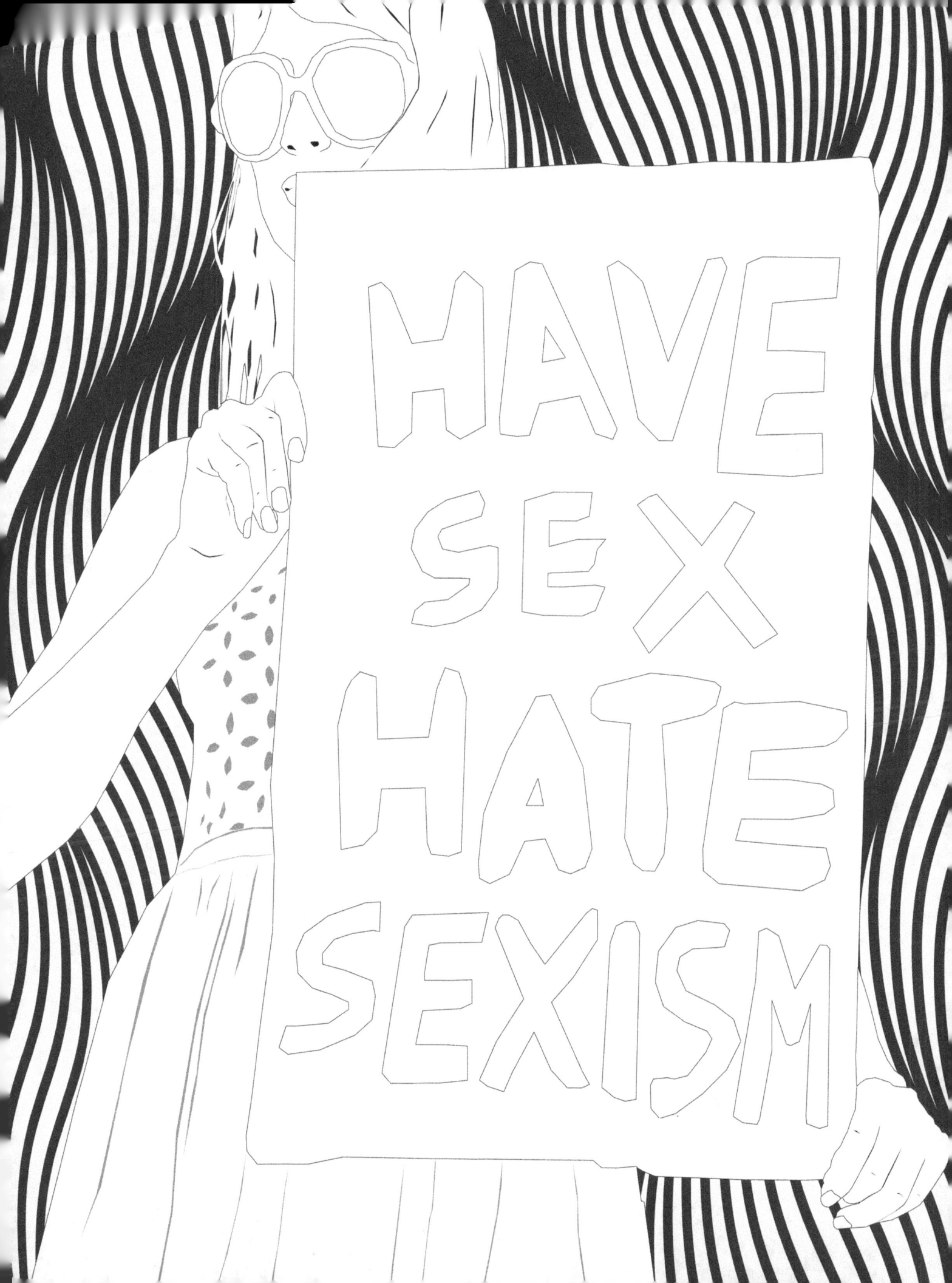

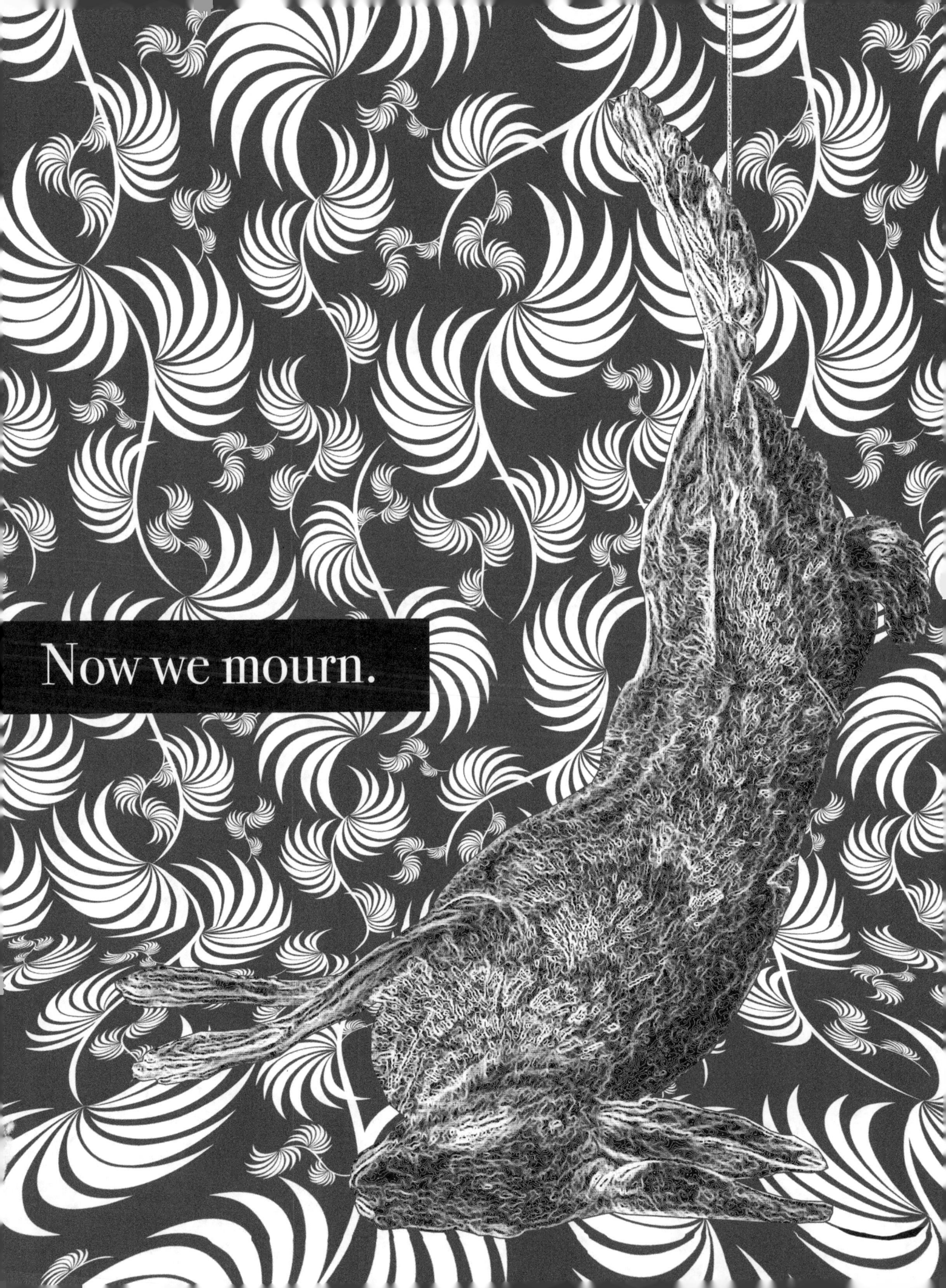

Now we mourn.

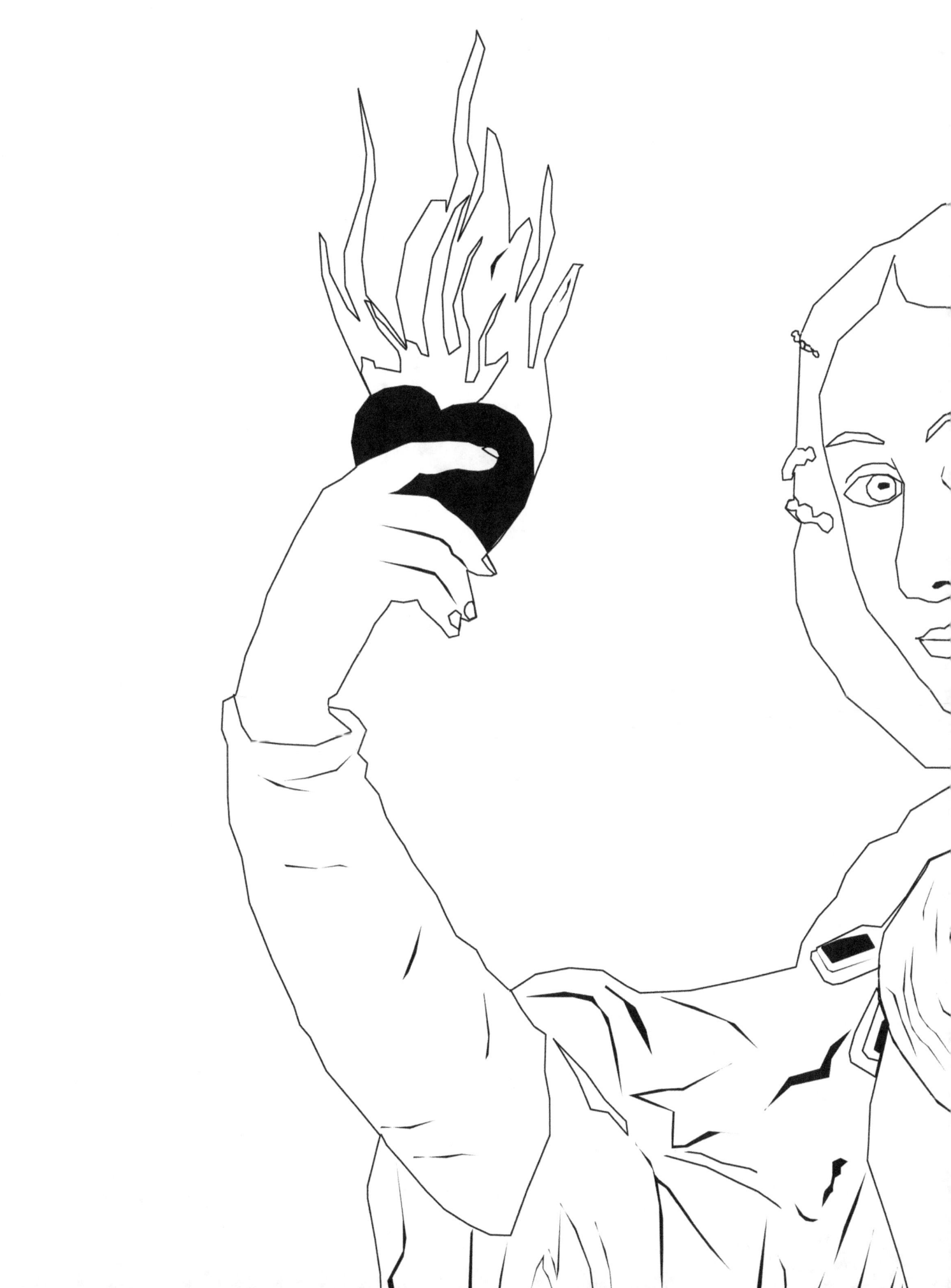

# IMAGE SOURCES

2. Original

3. Background- Original
   Cherub- Raphael, Galatea
   Foreground- Pietro da Cortona, The Rape of the Sabine Women

4. Background- Original
   Foreground- Pietro da Cortona, The Rape of the Sabine Women

5. Background- Cherubs from- Raphael, Galatea
   Foreground- Pietro da Cortona, The Rape of the Sabine Women

6. Background- Original
   Foreground- Jacopo ligozzi, Abduction of the Sabine Women

7. 19th C Engraving

8. Background- Rina Oshi/Shutterstock
   Foreground- Peter Paul Rubens, Rape of Daughters of Leucippus

9. Background- Jan Brueghel, The Earthly Paradise
   Foreground- Jacopo ligozzi, Abduction of the Sabine Women

10. Gaetano Cottafavi, Anfiteatro Flavio Detto il Colosso

11. CoolR/Shutterstock

12. Background- Jan Brueghel, The Earthly Paradise
    Foreground- Aarrows/Shutterstock

13. Foreground- Willem van Mieris, Susannah and the Elders
    Background- Jan Brueghel, The Earthly Paradise

14. Gian Lorenzo Bernini, The Rape of Proserpina

16. Adriaen van Oolen, Landscape with Birds

17. Background- Kynata/Shutterstock
    Foreground- David de Coninck, Rabbits, a Hare, and a Scarlet Macaw

18. Bernhard Anton Funke Kupper, A still life with a hare and poultry

20. Background- Aarrows/Shutterstock
    Foreground- Giovanni Battista Cipriani, The Rape of Orithyia

21. Background- Willem van Mieris, Susanna and the Elders
    Foreground- William-Adolphe Bouguereau, Charity

22. Background- Zubkova Iuliia/Shutterstock
    Foreground- Venetian School Allegory of Charity, circa 1700

23. Background: Kynata/Shutterstock
    Foreground: Meissen, The Rape of Proserpine

24. & 25. Giovanni Francesco Barbieri, Rinaldo Restraining Armida
         from Wounding Herself with an Arrow

26. Background- Ylianas/Shutterstock
    Foreground- Aarrows/Shutterstock

27. Background- Kynata/Shutterstock
    Foreground- Aarrows/Shutterstock

28. Background- Mur34/Shutterstock
    Foreground- Kaspars Grinvalds/Shutterstock

30. Anneka/Shutterstock

31. Background- 06photo/Shutterstock
    Foreground- Gian Lorenzo Bernini, Ecstasy of Beata Ludovica Albertoni

32. Gian Lorenzo Bernini, Ecstasy of Saint Teresa

34. Gian Lorenzo Bernini, Medusa

35. Background- Mur34/Shutterstock
    Foreground- Guido Reni, Lucretia

36. Background- Alex Tanya/Shutterstock
    Foreground- Artemisia Gentileschi, Susanna and the Elders

38. DreamBig/Shutterstock

39. Background- Tata_ota/Shutterstock
    Foreground- Antonio Canova, Venus Italica

40. Background- Kynata/Shutterstock
    Foreground- Photographee.eu/Shutterstock

42. & 43. Background- Sylvie Bouchard/Shutterstock
         Foreground- Giovanni Francesco Barbieri, Rinaldo
         Restraining Armida from Wounding Herself with an Arrow

44. Background- Zubkova Iuliia/Shutterstock
    Foreground- A Katz/Shutterstock.com

45. Background- Curly Pat/Shutterstock
    Foreground- Omasz Bidermann/Shutterstock

46. Background- Kynata/Shutterstock
    Foreground- Jan Weenix, Trophies of the Hunt

47. Francisco de Zurbarán, Allegory of Charity

In *Famous Rapes: From Mesopotamia to Steubenville*, author and artist Andrea Baker reflects on the history of how rape has been depicted. In *Famous Rapes: The Coloring Book*, Baker transforms her paper cutout art into a therapeutic adult coloring book. A portion of the profits from this book will benefit the District Alliance for Safe Housing in Washington, DC.

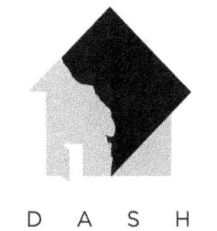

D A S H
DISTRICT ALLIANCE FOR SAFE HOUSING

Andrea Baker is an artist and writer. Her most recent full-length collection of poetry is *Each Thing Unblurred is Broken* (Omnidawn, 2015). She has been a Poetry Society of America Chapbook Fellow, and, in 2005, she was the recipient of the Slope Editions Book Prize for *Like Wind Loves a Window*. Her cut-out work has been featured in The Rumpus and anthologized in *Family Resemblance: An Anthology of Eight Hybrid Literary Genres* (Rose Metal Press, 2015). In addition to her work on the page, she is a subject in the documentary, *A Rubberband Is An Unlikely Instrument.* Her interest in visual and material culture is fed by her current employment as an appraiser of arts and antiques. She lives in New York City.

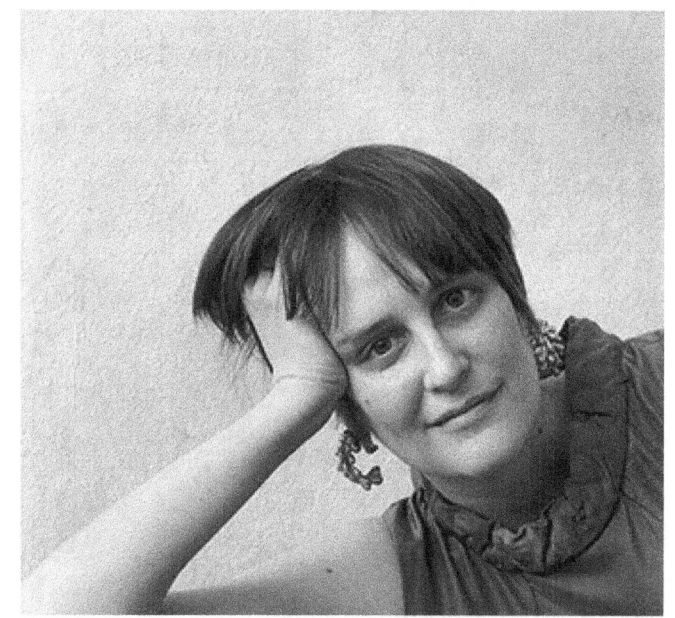

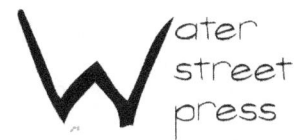

ater
street
press

www.waterstreetpressbooks.com

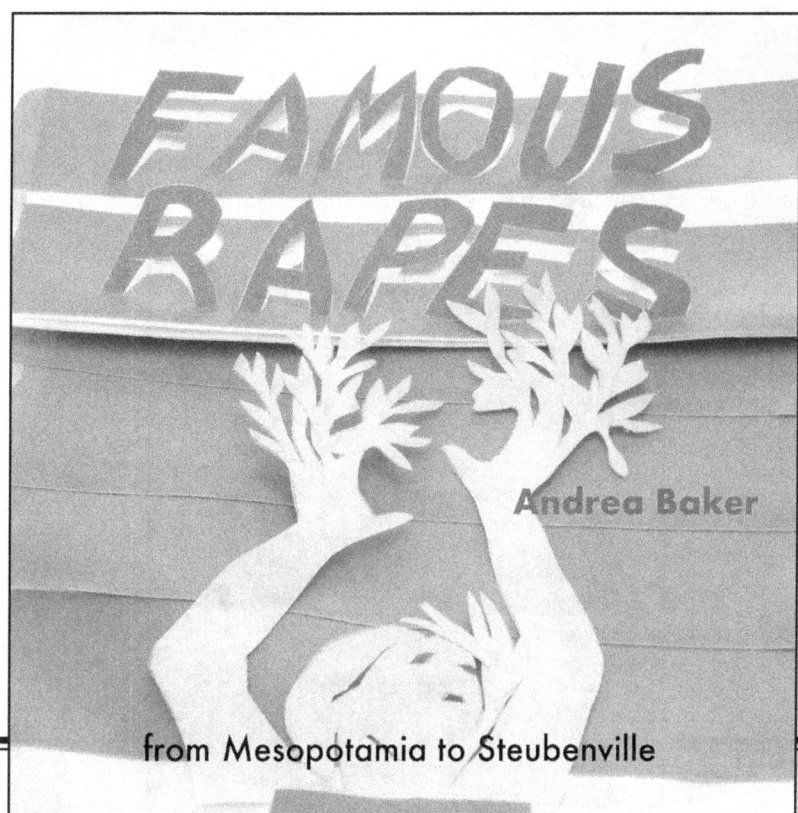

# FAMOUS RAPES
## BY ANDREA BAKER

It is a simple truth that throughout history, certain rapes have become "famous." Old Master painters depicted sexual violence again and again, generally representing it as the transcendent work of heroes. Traditional Catholic stories teach that it is better to die during an attempted rape than it is to survive a completed one.

In19th- and 20th-century America, notorious fear about the sexuality of black men wreaked havoc. From the days of Reconstruction through to the Central Park Jogger, wild accusations justified the literal and metaphoric lynching of men perceived as threats to white power.

Meanwhile, a revolution did take place. Conversations became public. Laws changed.

Andrea Baker's project is to reflect on the history of how rape has been depicted.

She draws images of sexual assault from both art history and contemporary visual culture, remaking them as spare white paper cutouts against a paper-packing-tape background. The swath of time from Mesopotamia to the present day is flattened and rolled out in unflinching continuity. As difficult as the material is, we do see progress within a history that is not always as distant we might prefer, and Baker is insistent that we celebrate our accomplishments, even as we continue to evolve.

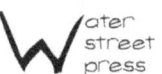

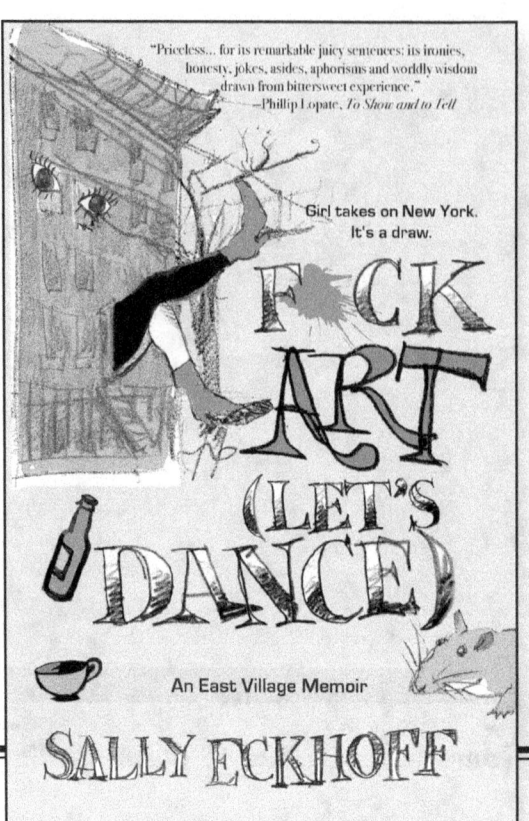

# F*CK ART (LET'S DANCE)
## BY SALLY ECKHOFF

*F*ck Art (Let's Dance)* is a chronicle of ten slam-bang years in a very slam-bang part of New York City, and of one young painter's crusade to make that place her own.

This memoir, by a former *Village Voice* writer and critic, starts in 1977 with the Summer of Sam and ends with the Tompkins Square Park riots—two notorious incidents that defined an age. After a last, desperate summer in the beach towns of Long Island, the naive young wannabe artist borrows her dad's El Camino, finances a trip to Manhattan with the change on his cufflink stand, and rents an apartment on East Tenth Street with a floor so crooked that everything that falls off the kitchen counter rolls under the bathtub. And then she begins to paint, eat, dance, and *feel* her way around New York.

*F*ck Art* might remind you of what it feels like to be a beginner in a land of crooks and geniuses.

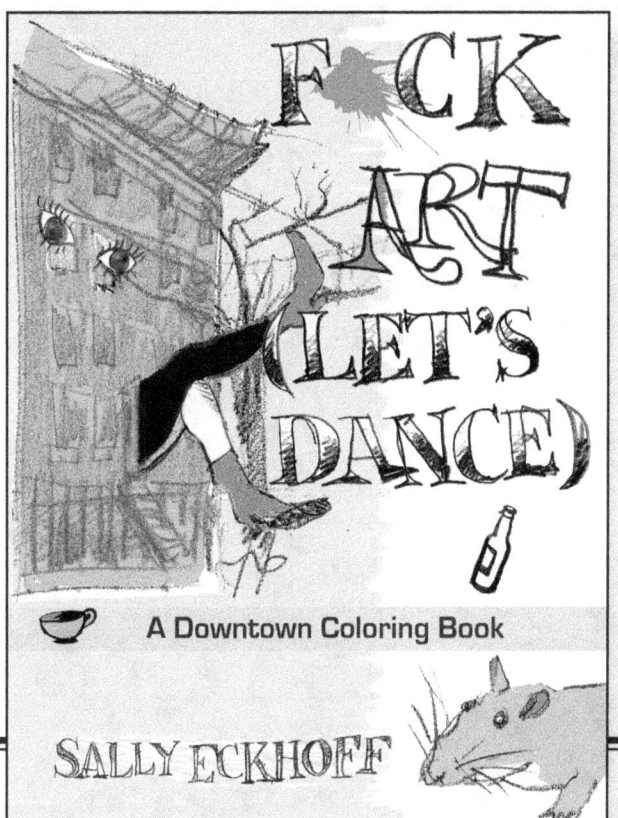

# F*CK ART (LET'S DANCE):
# THE COLORING BOOK
## BY SALLY ECKHOFF

In *F*ck Art (Let's Dance),* author and artist Sally Eckhoff told the story of the downtown art and music scene in New York in the last decade during which a starving artist could afford to eat (and sing and paint and dance) in Manhattan. *In F*ck Art (Let's Dance): The Coloring Book,* she recreates that scene as a punk art coloring book for adults.

Water Street press